A New Leaf
4

Also by Jim Gold

Books

Songs and Stories for Open Ears

Handfuls of Air: A Book of Modern Folk Tales

Mad Shoes: The Adventures of Sylvan Woods: From Bronx Violinist to Bulgarian Folk Dancer

Crusader Tours and Other Stories

Recordings

World of Guitar
American Folk Ballads

A New Leaf

4

Adventures in the Creative Life

Jim Gold

Full Court Press
Englewood Cliffs, New Jersey

First Edition

Copyright © 2005 by Jim Gold

All rights reserved. No part of this book may be
reproduced or transmitted in any form or by any means
electronic or mechanical, including by photocopying,
by recording, or by any information storage and retrieval system, without the express permission of the author,
except where permitted by law.

Published in the United States of America
by Full Court Press, 601 Palisade Avenue,
Englewood Cliffs, NJ 07632
fullcourtpress.com

ISBN 978-1-946989-52-9
Library of Congress Control Number: 2020904310

Editing and book design by Barry Sheinkopf

Table Of Contents

Writing, *1*

Languages, *13*

Life, *25*

Money and Its Brethren, *81*

Performance, *99*

Business, *121*

God, *189*

Inventions, *195*

Writing

Keep a notebook on my person. Always. Keep it strapped to my hand, shoulder, or side along with pens, calligraphy pens, and any other writing paraphernalia.

Write, write, write, in all languages, in all alphabets, in all scripts, in all ways, at all times.

Learn to draw. It improves not only eyesight and vision but gives a fresh, down to earth way of seeing.

On Redundancy and Repetition

Are parts of my *New Leaf Journal* redundant and repetitive?

Could redundance and repetitiveness be its strength? Is there unseen power in redundancy and repetition?

"Redundant" may be simply a negative term for the positive benefits of repetition?

Polishing the Jewels

Editing is a form of meditation.

I'm getting a sense of self-satisfaction and peace from it.

But the word itself is so mundane and dull.

Instead of "editing" I'll call it Polishing The Jewels.

This polishing is not a place of closure, frozen and fixed. Rather a temporary stop on the ascending ladder of spiritual evolution.

Enjoy the view! Then climb to the next rung.

Benefits of "You're Wonderful!"

I've taken the works of Eknath Easwaran and turned them on their head to make them fit me. He's given me cloth. I'm sewing a suit to fit my body, mind, and life style.

Let's take his idea of putting others first. I hate putting others first. I don't understand why anyone would want to do it. But I understand putting myself first very well. I believe self-interest rules behavior.

How could Easwaran and I get together?

In the "You're wonderful!" philosophy.

I heard four writers read their works at Hilda Bary's Poetry Reading in Bergenfield yesterday. All the readers were good but the last reader, Woody Rudin, was truly outstanding. His reading inspired me to improve myself.

During the afternoon reading I felt out of it, distant, blase, on the edge of closure. Michael sat next to me with his Indonesian girl friend. At the end of the reading he asked, "Are you going to read again?"

"I doubt it," I answered. "First I want to figure out what direction I'm heading in writing."

Michael turned to his girl friend. "This guy really has way out stuff," he said. "You'd like it. It's off-the-wall wonderful."

His words sent an electric shock through me. Suddenly, I felt awake and alert. Wonderful! Me? Hearing such a compliment knocked down my closure walls immediately and filled me an energy bordering on enthusiasm. Imagine, me wonderful! What a wonderful thought!

I reflected further. If I was feeling down, lackluster, and energy-less simply because I wasn't putting myself on the line by reading in public, and, if Michael's "You're wonderful!" words had energized me, what did these words mean?

Michael smiled. I could see it made him feel good to say I was wonderful. My being wonderful was making it wonderful for him. Something I had done, namely, give a service, read my work, express the creations of my inner life, not only made me feel whole and wonderful, but made him feel wonderful as well.

It feels so good when someone says, "You're wonderful!" Why would they say that? Because you are giving something to others. Putting others before you. Just what Easwaran says—only backwards. Your existence makes them feel good. That is why they say, "You're wonderful!" Often it has little to do with you and a lot to do with them. They have created, invented, imagined a situation, using your existence as ballast, which elevates them, makes them feel important, creative, and alive. They project it onto you. Nevertheless, despite this projection, you are still partly responsible for their feeling of wonderfulness.

Looking for a "You're wonderful!" in the deeper symbolic language of kabbalistic mysticism, mean: "I'm wonderful!" It is Martin Buber's "I And Thou" all over again.

Looking for that means you are unconsciously searching for a way to help others. On the surface, it can appear egotistic and narcissistic. But that is only a materialistic vision. The deeper explanation for this phenomenon is: When you shine in your existence the light you create shines on others.

Thus, Eknath Easwaran and I are both heading in the same direction—towards the truth of Self. He starts by thinking directly of— or through—others whereas I start by thinking directly of—or through—my self. His is the "intellectual" approach, mine the "artistic" one. Thus we driver on different roads to the same castle.

Writing As Meditation

I love the idea of writing as meditation. It is the right path for me. I have taken a step through the looking glass.

I write to understand myself, to dive into the inner sanctum and discover the well-springs, yearnings, and bottom lines of my being. What could that be but meditation? Indeed, I looked up meditation in the dictionary. It is related to the Latin word for medicine and beyond that to the Hebrew root mida meaning "to measure." Thus, I have been measuring myself for years, trying to fit myself into this world, figuring out where, how, and why I belong. I'm tailoring a suit of clothes to fit me, sweaters, jackets, pants, and shirts to fit my mind, good sturdy underwear to fit my body, fine hats, socks, and shoes to fit the spiritual longings of my soul. My "measuring days" began when I studied violin. What better way to measure? What better way to fit, squeeze, pull, and push through the meditation musical measures of life? Is my life in three quarter time? Am I a waltz clothed in flesh? A two fourths march? A parade displaying myself proudly before others, shoulders back, chest out, head high, marching up Riverdale Avenue showing my physical, mental, and spiritual wares before unsuspecting neighbors? Could I be a six-eighths jig with an Irish lilt to my style? As an adult, I discovered East European rhythms; Greek, Bulgarian, and Byzantine measures with seven, nine, eleven, even thirteen beats to a measure. Am I those? Do I meditate in off-beat rhythms too? Indeed, yes.

I have meditated all my life. A yoga of music, sound, and beauty.

What about breathing? I have been doing that all my life, too though I never called it pranayama. Will I discover a unique approach to breathing too?

Stay tuned to find out.

True Editing

Rethinking my thoughts as I rewrite them is true editing.

Judgements

It's so hard to judge whether my writing is good or not.

If I'm in the right mood, it's good. If I'm in the wrong mood, it's bad.

It may be simply impossible for me to judge my work.

I can't put my complete faith in others either since their judgements are subject to the same fickleness as my own.

I have to plough ahead, editing, and organizing my writing without judgements.

How is this done?

Writing

I read Jimenez in *Crusader Tours*. How could I have written such a book? Wild and imaginative! Clever, philosophical, and witty. Erudite and humorous. Wise and off-the-wall. It's all right there in front of me. Only I couldn't see it. Nor could I believe I wrote it.

But now I do.

Life of Crime

I read *When Jonny Comes Home*. A beautiful story.

It is a crime others have not read it. That beautiful story remains unnoticed.

I have a criminal past. What are my crimes?

1. Lack of faith in my talent.
2. Making little to no effort at bringing the fruits of my labor to the public.
3. Hiding my beautiful creations, thus robbing others of the opportunity to read them.

How Good It Is!

The hard part about reading and editing my 1995 *New Leaf Journal* is realizing how good it is! Not only does it read smoothly, easily and beautifully, but it is also filled with heart-warming wisdom.

Can I face such goodness? A positive answer to these questions is worth thousands of therapy dollars.

Maybe along with Torah, Hebrew, Hungarian, Buddhist, and yoga philosophical tracts, I should read my journals first thing in the morning.

Legacy

Daily, daily, I write.

I feel overwhelmed by the amount I am turning out. How will I edit all these pages? How will I publish them? They keep coming. Every day, more and more. An endless river. I'm happy for this abundance, but also overwhelmed.

The more I write, the easier it gets. Easy to pour the words over the pages, easy to let my mind wander wide and free, let my fingers roam, and let my feelings out. It is a blessing to write.

But in the back of my mind lurks the question: What will I do with it all? How will I prepare and present it to the public?

I know the answer: Publish book after book of these writings. If I average one book a year and I live to ninety, I'll end up with twenty-six volumes. Suppose I live to one hundred. That will make thirty-six volumes. And this does not include the 1994–2001 years. If I add these eight more it will be thirty-two volumes by age ninety, forty-two by one hundred.

Let's say that by the time I die, I produce forty volumes of these *New Leaf Journals*. Is forty so much? Averaging three hundred pages per book that makes three hundred times forty, equaling twelve thousand pages. Is twelve thousand too much? Will any reader wade through so many pages?

Not a good question to ask. After all, I've written books with less that sixty pages. This has not prevented people from not reading them. If people are interested, they will read whether a book is four pages or twelve thousand. Length is not the question, only interest. Will others be interested in what I write? Who knows?

It gets back to the personal. I am writing these books for myself. I am also publishing and producing them for myself. Naturally, I would like others to read them. I hope they are interested. But again, their interest is beyond my control.

Alone or not, my books are self-books, and their publication is self-publication. The process of writing them is a daily exercise in self-exploration. I want to publish them so that, when I die, I can stand before the Lord and say "Lord, I've done worthy work on Earth. I tried my best, gave life my strongest shot, stretched, pushed, and promoted the talents You gave me to their fullest."

I want to leave a legacy.

My books are my legacy. They are the fullest expressions of my mind without the presence of my body, the fullest expressions of my thoughts, dreams, wish, desires, feelings, and fantasies.

Legacy, you say. Are you leaving us?

No, I am not expecting to die. Sure, my body may shrivel into drivel, fade away, and disappear. But my body is not me.

Nevertheless, I want to leave a physical manifestation of my mental and spiritual self.

Editing My Own Books

If there is any work I have to do when I get back home from Prague and Budapest it is editing all my New Leaves.

I don't know if Barry will have time to do it all. Am I objective enough to do some myself? Will I cut out too much or leave too much in?

Stay tuned to find out.

Back To Four Pages a Day

I've been falling apart for the past few days. Or is it weeks... or months... (years?) I've become scattered as of late. (Or is it only a few days?) Lots of parenthesis, hesitancies, false starts here. I'm circling around a vital point. I'm back to writing four pages a day!

Isn't this where I started in 1994? Indeed, it is. At that time I hit on an enduring truth: Writing four pages a day keeps me sane and healthy. It energizes my mind, pumps my body, raises my spirit. I became a monastery within a monastery. Meaning and purpose entered my life every time I sat down to write.

Why have I stopped getting up at four a.m.? There was a time, not long ago, that rising four a.m. became a habit. Lack of sleep? The hell with it. I had a purpose. I didn't need to sleep that much. Besides, if I was tired, I could sleep in the afternoon. Post-luncheon naps made my day and fed my nights.

What is the answer to less sleep?

The answer to less sleep is more purpose! Inspiration must light your brain even while you sleep. Your desire to do something inspiring when you wake up must be so great that you can't wait for morning to come! When you lie down at night you think: Ah, in only four, five, or six hours, I'll be doing something I love! I can't wait for this sleep to be over. I can't wait to start! True love is waiting for me. I won't keep her long. Four to six hours of sleep is the absolute maximum time I can stay away from her.

My love is writing. I can't wait to jump out of bed and run into her arms! Why sleep when I can be with her? But, of course, one must sleep in order to survive. Survival comes even before writing. But writing answers the question of why bother surviving in the first place.

I am ready to return to a vengeance.

One thing that slowed down my writing was the "overwhelmed" idea. I produce so many pages. How will I ever manage to edit them all? Even though Barry has edited the *New Leaf Journals* of 1994—

1996, three journals, we still have not done 1997 to 2001. That's five years of unedited journals to go. And I'm still producing! At this rate, I'll never get finished, never have closure on my writing. But closure may not be the purpose of my writing. It may be an open ended thing, going on for the rest of this life. I'll just keep producing, page after page. Yes, they may all die with me.

Stop thinking about immortality and the future. It is idolatry; they are false idols. I am a monotheist. I connect to my one God during the writing process. That is where and how I worship. Worry about becoming overwhelmed is hubris and idolatry even though it may be hubris and idolatry on a "higher" level.

I must face the fact that my writing I will never be finished. Finished means death. But even that major annoyance can't stop me. There is always rebirth and reincarnation.

Well, I'm tired now.

But I've knocked out three pages. Well, who is counting? Me, of course. Why? Because numbers drive me on. I've got one more page to go. Producing it will push me higher.

I feel complete, full, and healthy again.
I'm back to writing!

Starting Over

Old words return, worn-out phrases and distance marmalade passages. I've said and done it all before. Even that is a tired and worn out phrase. But I have no other way of beginning. True, all my phrases, words, and flying turds may be thrown out later. Indeed, I ought to clean out this page. But nevertheless, a turpentine is ramming. I can feel the latent energy deep in my bones, twisting my marrow, driving the turbine engine of herculean fortitude deep into my personal Tora Bora cave. No Afghanistan here, nor Al Qaeda either. All personal normal modern daily political and contemporary words. I don't know where to begin. But I also do know. I know I must begin the pouring process again with its delete, throw out, and discarding of entire pages.

Today my writing is stiff, tried, overdone, undercooked, cliché-filled, and this with my own clichés. I cannot write fresh. No fresh ideas in mind. Only the need to return to the past—which, of course, I can never do. But I need the remembrance of former juices, of four-page a day energy cycle. I have lost all sense of purpose and reason for existence. I see no future. I've "done it all." My days are over, numbered, finished, caput. Old ways are down the drain. I see no new ones up ahead, or even around me. I hope to discover something new as I write. It has helped clean me out in the past. Will it do its magic again? Will writing lift, not only the heavy cloud over my head and help me discover a new reason to exist?

I've succeeded in playing the guitar, finishing therapy, writing hundreds of pages. I'd like to have them published and have hundreds of readers clambering at my door, wanting to read, read, read my books. Suppose that happens. Suppose hundreds by my books, in fact, everything I've ever written, is gobbled up by an eager public. How would it make me feel? Wonderful! But then as I imagine further, I see the wonder passing. Soon I get used to adulation, the money rolling in and the number of readers rising. Finally, I am back to the "What else is new?" question.

I am not knocking success. The dream of mucho readers would obviously be nice, lovely, and wonderful. It would make me very happy. . . for awhile.

At least I hope it would make me happy for awhile. Am I rationalizing away all the sales work that has to be done to promote my writing? Probably. I hate to think of all the work it takes to be merely accepted, published, and promoted in the outside world. Can't they just accept, love, and publish me without this torture?

Deep down I realize I will never promote my work with the energy born of desperation that I once promoted my concerts. At the moment, I am not desperate enough. I am merely dissatisfied. That is not enough for true motivation.

But its cloud is enough to make me write. The writing process is fundamental to my existence. I can never get away from it. Nor do I want to. Writing fulfills all or most of my dreams.

I must write for my own satisfaction, sanity, self-exploration, and self-knowledge; I must write to discover my purpose, meaning, sparks, and place in the universe. Writing puts me next to, into, the God within. We're a team who work well together.

What I am saying above has been said it countless times before in countless journal pages. I have no new message to give.

Yet I must write it, say it. keep reminding myself over and over again.

Freedom and Protection Walk Together

Code names disguise my characters. Changing their names protects me... and them. But they still retain their personal meaning and value.

Protection not only protects everybody, but, on the more positive side, frees me to write about anything and anyone I want! Freedom and protection walk together.

Spreading Wonders Throughout the World

Nothing cures like writing, like pouring out page after page. Pour, pour, pour. Who cares whether I repeat myself? Repetition is an illusion. Every day I start a new life. I may repeat words and even ideas, dance the same steps over and over, play the same Alhambra, do the same calliyoga routine, eat the same foods, run the same routes: All this may seem like repetition. But, in actuality, it is dynamic new-day approach whirling through one world, ever different even as it appears to be the same. What a credo! New swirling in old forms, ancient and modern in eternal embrace. New forms may emerge. But disguised and hidden within them dwell an ancient energy.

It doesn't matter what I write. It is only important that I write. Over and over again. Repetition becomes diversity wearing new clothing. A new suit looks good on the old body.

Where will all this lead? Nowhere. In that familiar yet foreign land of Nowhere, there is always somewhere to turn, and someone to turn to. Even if these are figments of imagination, nevertheless, their stark virtual reality bodes well for the errant mind. It plants firm ballast underneath the wandering sail.

Words are coming, streaming, flowing over the page, helter skelter, to and fro, unstoppable, unbeatable, ringed in truth, sweltering in marble and marmalade tops, dikospheres punctured in semi-platitudinous wirebouts. Nonsense marches on.

New Leaf is an adventure story. A voyage of self-discovery. Columbus crossing the self-understanding ocean. Editing its contents is a technicality, important but secondary.

My Message

An audience for *New Leaf Journal* is other writers. My message is: Everyone should write a journal. It is so good for your mental, physical, and spiritual health!

Poetry

Edit my journal down, down, down to its bare essence.
Turn *New Leaf* into poetry. This can be done through slow, careful, conscious, caring editing.

Writing as Part of Breath and Life

I had nothing to write today. I still turned out four pages. Writing has become so much a part of my breathing, daily routine, and life, that I hardly notice the pages I turn out.

Languages

Bursting In "Hiriq" Freedom

In ancient geocentric times, earth was seen as the center of the universe. It's astronomic symbol was a dot, a Hebrew vowel *hiriq*.

When man is stuck in *hiriq*, stuck in the center of the earth, he lies in the "coffin of responsibility."

This vowel has two qualities: Stuck, frozen in place, or roaring through the universe in a burst of freedom. As in the dual meaning and personality of hiriq, one can either lie at the center of the earth surrounded by darkness in a limbo coffin of responsibility, or stand, surrounded by everlasting light, at the center of the universe bursting in freedom.

> Hebrew Is Clicking!
> Hebrew is clicking!
> Hours of daily study suddenly paid off.
> It pays to practice!
> Put in hours of unrequited time.
> Daily, daily, daily,
> Patiently, patiently, patiently
> No hope of reward
> Following the path
> Until one day
> The window of illumination opens.
> For a delicious moment
> I understand!
> And fluttering wings of purple glory
> Shine in the Light.

It's Not Easy Being A Word

Latin is a highly inflected language riddled with declension.

Nouns, pronouns, adjectives, and verbs are inflected, bent out of shape, twisted, perverted, and diminished.

So diminished are they, that inflection is called declension—a deterioration, descent, sloping, falling away. A decline.

Declension shows case, number, and gender.

Case, from the Latin cadere—to fall, is another "case" of diminishment. Here words are twisted beyond their true selves, partially stripped of their essential nature; they are pushed, forced, and enslaved, squeezed into strange forms to become subjects, objects, and possessors,

They can also lose their individuality and identity by being reduced to mere numbers—another form of debasement. Or they can be twisted and turned on the gender rack.

Changes in a verb are called conjugation. Thus verbs are better off than nouns, pronouns, and adjectives. They might even see marriage in their future along with conjugal visits. However, verbs can be tense and suffer from mood changes, schizophrenic shifts of person, voice difficulties, and even the same number problems as their noun, pronoun, and adjective cousins.

It's not easy being a word.

If you want to be tough, strong, and stable, be a noun.

But if you want to be mobile, be a verb.

Infinity and Limitations

"Infinitives" soar. Soaring opens limitless flight through the heavens.

Finite forms express limits. They are found in conjugations: *I soar, you soar, he, she,* or *it soars*. First personal singular, "through the masks of sameness," (First—from Latin *"per"* through; masks from Latin *"persona"* mask. Singular from Latin, *"singularis"* and Hebrew *"semel,"* same, similar.)

The same limitations apply to plurals.

Crossing the Tourist Desert

I read that Moses wanted to bring everything he owned—"not one hoof will remain"—out of Egypt. He didn't know what he'd need to serve God in the desert. Like a tour leader, he was situational: he'd know what method or tool to use when he got there. And, like a tour leader, he wanted to bring as much equipment from home to use "just in case."

I do the same thing when I leave home to lead a tour. I bring as many props "out of Egypt" as I can: computer, writing books, language and history books, all to help me survive in the tourist desert.

Perfection is a path not a place.

Reading Slowly

Slowly I read about Moses in Hebrew. I spent an hour on two sentences. At this rate, it will take sixty lifetimes, if not more. to finish the Torah.

What about crossing the desert and reaching the Promised Land, reaching that place of rest and closure where I can say "Look at me folks, I finally made it!" I'll never get there. The more I read, the slower I read. Slow, slow, slow. True, I go deeper into each sentence, word, and vowel sign; I wring out meanings from each letter. Yet, I am pursued by a fleeting "I'll never finish this thing no matter how hard I try," panic.

Can I accept studying or practicing something I'll never finish? Can I accept my daily slide into the abyss of eternity, the terrifying vision of the infinite?

I am hung on the cross. The horizontal pantibulum is pain, the vertical stipiti is pleasure. As I hang daily, tied to the crossbars, dogs devour my feet and birds peck out my eyes. In three days of less I will die of suffocation.

What else can I do? Is there really a choice?

I'll never finish Torah study in this lifetime or many more. Yet, I want to finish.

What does "finish" mean?

Reaching an ecstatic moment of awareness where All is One.

The Next Mountain To Climb

I sat on the side of the road in Taormina, Sicily, thinking: I need a new mountain to climb.

What upcoming projects shall I embrace?
1. Spain for May of 1999
    a. A guitar, dance, and southern Spain tour.
2. Study Latin languages along with history.
    a. Climb the Tour-Language-History mountain.
Find new mountains in yoga, guitar, and writing.

When the Climbing-The-Next-Mountain attitude flashed through me, I felt electrified. It filled me with energy and enthusiasm, a power and desire to pursue endless possibilities.

I would be happy is such explosive, volcanic Mount Etna approach guided my entire existence. I can think of nothing better.

The-Next-Mountain-To-Climb attitude is a fitting climax to my tour of Sicily and Rome.

Dacian Rumblings

I have returned. The doors are burning down and the cat is crazy running out of the house. My bowels are in an uproar and the furnace is lit with kerosene from distant Byzantine lamps. Only catcalls and caterwauls are flying backwards tonight even though it is morning.

I work directly with my God connection. Finally, it makes sense. Years of reading, studying, learning, dying, rebirthing, living in the stylistic light of backward and past years are slowly and steadily beginning to pay off. Yes, folks, I do meditate after all! I have been doing it for years; nay, most of my life. But I didn't know it was meditation. I called it art.

It any case, by simply turning a few words around, I find I am easily following all the dictates of post-menopausal meditation of the fornicating ant variety practiced by members of the pre-historic Module civilization living on the banks of the Danube. These ancient warmongers, comfortably nested in Danubian sands, forebears of the noble Dacian leader, Decebelus, practiced archery well before the Roman conquest. In later days, from his capital in Sarmogethusae, Decebelus diplomatic strung up fosters well with the Roman emperor, Domitian. Sarmogethusae, you say. And how do you spell that fucker, anyway? Is it Sarmogethusae, Sarmozegethuse, or what? I raced to look it up. Sarmizegethusa! That's it. It marches well with the first Dacian War, too. Decebelus won that diplomatic battle only later to lose to emperor Trajan. Victory column of Trajan, indeed. And to think I almost saw it in Romania last year. I should visit Sarmizegethusa once in my life. Imagine standing on the ground of the ancient Dacian capital; imagine Decebelus sitting on his throne, drinking Dacian wines, robbing the clitoral wine-pressings of virgins along with their social security numbers, and raising his third finger to Roman domination before succumbing to the ultimate Latinization of his language. What is Dacian and who are the Dacians, anyway? A Thracian tribe related to the Getae, of course.

After this brief foray into the back wards of history I am returning to my present God connected writing. Indeed, it is a pleasure to let the words fly across the pages again.

Mount Vesuvius belching smoke. Pumice ash raining down on helpless twats, vaginas gone wild with sea scum pumped from the volcanic eruptions on the island of Stromboli. Lying on Stromboli's beach, far from the Roman crowd, I wonder at the sight of distant Eolian islands lite by smoke, fire, and floating ashen chips their only hope beyond Roman baths is the Church of Saint Peter whose Vicoli chains never make it beyond the horns of Michelangelo's Moses.

Visiting The House Of Historical Loves

Yesterday I went to Barnes and Noble; I bought the *Rough Guide to Italy* and A *Historical Atlas Of Ancient Rome*. The Rough Guide series are the best guide books. I'm enthusiastic about the *Historical Atlas,* a musical, mystical, historical, dream adventure as are most history books. Indeed, to me, history is a dream adventure with "real" historical characters leading the drama. History is a dream. I love dreams. I can't get Calderon's *La Vida Es Sueno* out of my head. Although I've never read it, the ephemeral mystery of its title haunts me. Like the cloud of the Lord hovering over the Israelites as they crossed the desert, the dream is my cloud above me, ever pointing in the right direction, protecting me from a destructive concrete vision that sees life as a permanent material reality. Yes, as Calderon said, *La vida es sueno*—Life is a dream. I love it that way. My philosophy is: Keep dreaming! Dreams are much closer to reality than the material existence of so-called "real" life events.

I rarely talk about my love of books. Is it lack of self-esteem, a holdover from my school days where I was a mediocre student, and spend most of my time in class daydreaming? My marks stunk. Sometimes I managed to get them out of the stink hole. But even with all my effort I could only raise them to average. I was never a good student in school. However, if you measured my dream capacity, my ability to fantasize in class, I would have gotten straight A's.

I still have a poor self-image as a student. Thus, how can I dare speak of lofty ideas, wondrous, miracle filled tombs of history, philosophy, language, and whatever? I love to read these masterful books, to bathe in their visions and ideas. I approach study as bather. I swim in the ocean of learning. But bathers often get poor marks in school. How dare I, a bather, speak of lofty historical ideas! What is my pedigree?

Turning Anger Into Compassion

Turning anger into compassion means turning shit into fertilizer.
Turn the shit others throw at you into garden fertilizer. Some day you'll thank them for helping your flowers grow.

Yoga Morning

Primal energy emanating from the loins
Connects me with the animal world.

Learn to be grateful for opposition.

Stop at the beauty moment.

"The Little Russian Teacher Within"

I have no Russian teacher. When a Russian language problem comes up I'm forced back into myself. I have to look to the "Little

Russian teacher within" to find the answer. I didn't know I had a "Little Russian teacher within" but I do.

How did I find this out? Well, after thinking enough about my Russian language problems, suddenly, to my surprise, the answers appear!

For example, after reading decyat dnei—ten days, I asked myself why the ending of den (in the nominative case) was *ei, dnei*? I knew something about numbers taking the genitive case. I looked up all case endings but found no confirmation of this thought. Then I realized that Russian numbers take the genitive, but up to five they take the genitive singular while after five and up to twenty, they take the genitive plural! Aha! I looked up the plural ending for soft masculine words such as den which end in the soft sign, and voila, it was indeed *ei*, or *dnei*.

Another victory for the "Little Russian teacher within."

Drill, drill. Knock the genitive in. Look up those Russian noun endings, those case endings, over and over. Pound them into my head. I want to look them up, fall back into their loving arms, scurry back into the arms and cuddle at the breast of mother Russia, mother Grammar, the secure, didactic, and structured.

I like the womb of mother Russia. Her palatalizing sounds make me feel warm and secure. I love her soft palate on my cheek, the rolling of beautiful Russian sounds on my tongue, pressing softly against cheek and palate, making me feel round and secure in this fuzzy, sharp-pointed world.

Ah, A Nominative!

An accusative case accuses you all day.

The world is full of accusatives. One learns to live with them. What else can you do?

But a nominative names you. It stands up for you. Nominatives are accepting mothers! Ah, how I love the nominative case!

Language Is the Path into My Soul

A prime purpose of my tours is to give me the opportunity, motivation, and inspiration to study.

Study what?

Language and culture... But mostly language.

Language has the sound of history, the tone of culture. It is the source of my inspiration. This study is above money making. Money will come "by itself" if I follow the right path. But first, I must believe in my path.

Language is the path into my soul.

Follow it!

Learning to speak Arabic is good.

Learning to write, read, and draw it is even better!

Budapest

I am in Budapest, sitting in my Artotel room overlooking the Danube, suffering from jet lag, and feeling awful.

Can such negative feelings be used to raise me up?

Yes! Witness how it fertilized the exciting idea of carrying the Bible, Hungarian grammar book, and Hungarian-English, English-Hungarian dictionaries on my person at all times! Also, to write my hand-written journal in Hungarian.

Beyond this is the idea of carrying books in Hebrew, Hungarian, Arabic, even Bulgarian on my person at all times. Yes, why not make mastering these languages a daily lifetime project!

I can start the practice today.

Hungarian (and some Hebrew through my Hungarian-Hebrew Torah) will be my next ten-day project. In Prague, I'll add Czech.

The music of language rings the bell of eternity.

Studying languages, keeping linguistic books on my person at all times, constantly referring to them and studying their contents, is my way of staying in touch with these higher forces on a daily basis.

Learn a foreign word or foreign sentence a day. Actually, it is to memorize a foreign word, a "word of the day." The sentence is to memorize its usage.

Why do I want to accumulate this useless knowledge? Why put in the daily effort to improve my linguistic skills? Why the endeavor?

It is to wake up the fervor and ignite the passion on a daily basis. It is to make contact with the infinite stream, the pulsating flow, the magnanimous hiking, the Sinai sinuvial, the fertile Nile alluvial plain, the nasal passages, the caves of intent located deep in the mind. On and on. It is to be in touch with higher forces on a daily, permanent basis.

Now, of course, the outward form of this endeavor is the apparently useless task of merely memorizing a word. But, in the trying, in the maximum effort, comes the contact with the Ineffable Stream, a touch of the divine.

Not a bad way to start the daily cycle.

Begin each day by trying. Making that maximum effort.

Four Words A Day

New language program: Learn four words a day. In one, two, or three languages. Learn the same words in Hebrew. . .and Hungarian.

Four a day. Every day a new four.

What a good thing to do with my mind. Instead of letting it wander distracted by external events, and in vacant uselessness, train it to focus on four new words a day.

Re Correct Verbs

"It's important to speak Spanish correctly."
"Why?"
"Because it is important to be understood."
"Why? Even when I speak English I am often not understood."

This proves that the bottom line in language is to have fun speaking. If others happen to understand you, so much the better.

Life

Creating My Own Perfume

Love is creativity.

Creativity is exactly what has been missing in my business. In the past, I saved it for the arts. That's where it "belonged." Business was crass, materialistic affair performed only by bourgeois boors. A true communist did not "do" business; nor did any person of refinement, culture, and education, or intellectuals, professors, or artists. They may have been supported by money from business, and, in actually, they were a business. But they refused to see it that way. What good communist would? They were too self-righteous to recognize any contribution except from working class people, and this even though they rarely knew any of the proletariat personally.

Creativity never went with business. This was a given. Everything in the communist world was neatly sliced up: art and creativity for artists; brain work and intellect for professors, and intellectuals. The world of my communist childhood was divided into good and evil. Good belonged to the proletariat; The concept of "goodness" was explained to them by the intellectuals who "really knew how things worked." Capitalists were bad. Business people personified evil.

I had lots of strikes against me when I wanted to become an artist. Being creative was okay, that's what artists did. But trying to make money at it was definitely out of the question. Earn money? Make a living from art? How dare you pollute the very spirit of creation itself! Money and art, shit and perfume: putting them together was like pouring Chanel Number 5 into a cesspool.

Such self-defeating, anti-entrepreneurial attitudes gave me a sour start. But I followed my route anyway because I couldn't stand being told what to do. I'd rather mix shit with perfume than give up my dreams of independence, creation, and a free artistic soul.

After twenty years of wandering in the deserts of artistic and business conflict, I'm finally reaching a new business neighborhood. I've resolved my conflict between creativity and business by combining them. I'm ready to mix shit with perfume and fertilize new flowers. I'll create a new perfume called Shitel Number 5.

Cry Baby

Tom Morgan went to Syms department store. Before he began shopping he sat down in a corner.

"I am frustrated, pissed-off, and sad," he said. "When will this misery end? I just want to rear back on my hind legs and complain! Woe, woe, woe. Poor me. I want to milk every misery for eternity. Yes, I feel sorry for myself, real sorry. Why don't I have a good life? Why can't I have what I want? Why must people be so selfish and only think of themselves? Why are they so much like me? Can't they be selfless, good, and kind and send me money because I want it? Why don't they register for my excellent services?

"These services are my gift to others. I want to give. . . but where are these "others" I want to give to hiding? I don't see any of them around. Please show up. How can they be so inconsiderate? What is wrong with them, anyway? Can't they see how wonderful I am?

They say in times of trouble, turn to God. Well, where is He? I don't see Him either. I don't see any customers coming from Him. Maybe I need a new agent.

They're all against me. Paranoid, you say. I'm not paranoid. I'm right. Nobody wants me. Poor, poor me. Sure, I'm a big baby. Are you trying to criticize me for "acting" like a baby? Who says I'm acting? The question arises: is my babyhood permanent or transient state? Well, who cares? I don't. But if I think about it, it doesn't feel transient at all. I am a baby. . . and proud of it! An adult in diapers. I'm proud of that, too. I bought my diapers in Syms Department Stare. They are the best! You say I misspelled Store by calling it Stare instead. Well, that was no mistake. When you try on diapers in Syms, and then walk around the store wearing them, everyone stares!

I'm crying. Tears are streaming down my cheeks. I'm so forgotten and neglected. I'm a good looking baby. Why don't those morons in the store see this? Can't they notice me? Can't they see I'm just a baby disguised as an adult? Why are they all so dense?

Every frustration is a challenge.

Moses Chases The Rats Away

I lost my way on the magic study path with its linguistic branches of Arabic writing, Hebrew script, Cyrillic flow, Hungarian juggernauts, Bulgarian, Turkish, and Greek twists, and even unknown Lithuanian. A wall has been erected between love and obligation.

All this is nothing new. I'm repeating myself. Even my writing is repetition to the extent that everything I'm saying is a rehash of old stuff. Is it getting boring? I'm saying the "same thing" on a new level. I continue to write, pouring it out non-stop to cleanse my soul. The more I do, the madder I get; the madder I get, the cleaner I become. . . and the better I feel! As I write straight, pure, and directly into the computer, waves of life-giving juice creep back into my body. Writing is doing its salvation work, restoring and revitalizing me. Sitting at the morning computer, coffee in hand, my fingers pour over the keys. Words flow.

I just want to write, write, write. All day long. Write until I drop. Never stop. I want the jumping juices to flow again. Free me from prison. Release me from the vice-like grip of double terror fears rolling down the mountain, from cascading fountains of water mules kicking and screaming behind burning Sinai bushes. Rodents scatter before the fiery commandments of Moses ben Rodent. What did Moses say to them? It's a great mitzvah to be filled with joy. Those words alone made the rats scatter and scamper. Scurrying like crazy, tails between their legs, they fled the burning bush and raced southward. Leaving Sinai's Magic Mountain behind, they searched for ratholes, caves, and hiding places in the Negev desert.

Rats can't stand up to joy.

Moses had the light. Or was it fire in his eyes? Moshe's ocular searchlight illuminated the joyless path; his radiant vision burned holes through grey black rodent furry coats. Poison, rat-juice, joyless life drained from their dying mouths. Carcasses of depression, gloomy intestines, and bilious wastes lay scattered over the road to Mount Sinai. The pungent odor of burning rat bodies filled the air.

Mental toughness helps you live as a tough nut of compassion in a hard world.

My Soul Dwells in the Universal Soul

I feel so good this morning! How long this feeling will last I do not know. But no matter what happens to it, some wonderful decisions have been made.

I'm reading the bible.

The bible takes personal emotions and universalizes them. It is talking about feelings, psychotherapy, oneness, but in a universalized way. Substitute your name for Israel or Moses and the bible becomes a very personal read, a journey into your soul.

My soul dwells in the universal soul.

Kosovo

Leave the Serbs and Albanians alone. It is their war, their business. Respect their right to fight it out among themselves, even if they kill each other in the process. The so-called liberal attitude that "I must help you even if you don't want my help, even if my help makes things worse," is totally arrogant. "Your life causes me so much pain that I must interfere in it; I must help you because I know better than you." Ugh, ugh, ugh! This attitude makes me want to vomit.

Recognition means respecting my right to do things my way. And this even though you think my way is the wrong way.

Beauty Must Be Top Priority!

As I wade piles of details and a heap of annoyances, remember: Beauty must be top priority!

I fell into the abyss of financial worry and temporarily forgot what I was all about. Such concerns made me forget the beauty of Tunisia. I lost the vision of studies, the joy of learning, beauty of Arabic, French, Spanish, history, camel riding in the Sahara desert at Douz, the Saharian Atlas, Tamerza, Tozeur, and more.

Why bother living if one forgets beauty? Beauty is what I am all about. Everything else is a footnote.

Jews say, Forget Israel and you are lost. I say, Forget Beauty and

I am lost. Israel is Beauty and vice versa. Such Beauty is found off the coast of Tunisia on the island of Jerba.

Such beauties of our Tunisian tour! How stars shone creating Islamic revelations that "souk" me to my foundations. The beauy of Arabic script, learning a new Arabic word, speaking French, shining strolls on the Hammamet beach, a beautiful Tunisian face. Why worry about debts, and other concerns that plague me? Yes, these are problems, but they are minor compared to the great darkness, pain, and sin of forgetting Beauty. Surviving in the material world will always be a problem. Nevertheless, survival is my skill.

Aside from minor problems, I've got a life style filled with significant moments. The sun shines most of the time. I love my tours, dance classes, writings, studies, and all the other factors found in my miracle schedule. How could I possibly give up such a life style merely to get out of debt, or make lots of money? Sure like bricks in the walls of a house, they're important. Without them I'd have lots of holes for the wind and rain to go through. This make life uncomfortable at times. But the discomfort is nothing compared to the vital crash into the grave taking place when I forget my mentor, Grand Muse, and Leader, Mrs. Beauty who reigns supreme in my life. She is the center of my house. Who cares if a few holes get blown in the walls or even if I have to live with permanent or long-time holes. If I remember my Beauty Muse, I'm on solid ground, safe and secure on my foundation.

Remember Beauty. Then to have the courage to stick to her no matter what!

Birthday Thoughts

Today is my birthday.
I am certainly younger than I was a few years ago.

Could Alexander Bellow, my second guitar teacher, have been wrong about his relaxation technique? I had to spend twenty-three years to find out I had been right in the first place. Bellow said: "Do it my way. It is the right way, the Segovia way, the only way." I've been trying to play his "right way" his ever since.

My first guitar teacher, Rolando Valdes-Blaine, had the best idea. Basically, he said, do it your own way.

Dare To Be Positive

I am a positive thinker. By nature, even after hitting bottom, I come up with a positive approach to life. Otherwise how could I survive in my own business. Positivism is one of my basic instincts.

Yet it has often been suppressed. Why?

When it rises, I hear old critical voices telling me such positivism is naive, unsophisticated, and stupid. Positive thinkers are fools. They are afraid to face the "reality" of the hard, negative, and oppressive world around them.

These are the cynical voices of the "sophisticates" I grew up worshiping. They had answers. They knew it all. I admired their certainty, their so-called knowledge of how the "real" world works. How could you beat their combination of cynical, smart, razor-sharp intellect and thorough knowledge of Marxism. What chance did my miniature positivism, nurtured in the secret confines of my room, fed by beautiful violin playing and celestial music, have against these powerful but cynical intellectuals? My tiny voice, even if it dared to pipe up, would only be squashed under an avalanche of "you stupid fool!" and other slashing criticisms. So my secret positive self lay hid in the closet while my public self knelt at the feet of false gods.

Cynics were smart. Positive thinking was naive and stupid. The "smart" person was on guard and most often negative. That was the "right" way to look at the world.

I see the cynics living in my brain, shouting me down, heil-Hitlering their destructive dictates. They are not me. Who are they? Foreign invaders living in and taking control of my brain.

Be myself. Dare to be positive!

Motivating Others, Motivate Myself

In Latvia, as we sat in Riga's Zem Abeles restaurant, Lillian asked: "What do you offer in a tour?"

I thought a long moment, then answered: "Good question. What do I offer?" I paused, then took a long sip of beer. "My desire to run this tour. I offer a high-panting philosophy of Enthusiasm First. Then, after enthusiasm, I offer more enthusiasm with a touch of divine madness. If you're not full of God, who cares what else you're full of?"

Influencing

I filed through my old papers I came across the letterhead of George Dauphinais, a businessman who loved classical guitar. I met him in Springfield, Illinois, after I gave a concert there. He ended up flying in all the way to Teaneck, New Jersey, for guitar lessons with me. Then began to sell fine classical guitars from his home in Springfield. I wonder what became of him. It brought back many memories of the college and community concert period of my life.

It's frightening, humbling, and beautiful to think of all the people I have influenced over the years. How important I have been to them.

This shows how important it is to publish my writing, record my songs, get them out of my mental and physical basement, bring them public to influence and effect others. It is so hard to remember that I am important. But, since I am, it is important that I offer the important parts of myself to others.

Long-Range Thinking

Cells and muscles in my body experience the growing pains of long range thinking. Essentially long range thinking is optimistic thinking. Eventually, I'll do what has to be done. "Eventually" may mean days, months, years, even life times. But, the end result will nevertheless be success. Short term thinking is second-place thinking.

Long range thinking is first-place thinking.

War!

Old cells die; new ones are born. My body aches.
For what purpose?

War!

I need an excellent body to fight this war. Running, yoga, and calliyoga exercises train the body keeping it in shape for the struggle.

Art forms are my knives, guns, and bombs. Writing, guitar playing, and folk dancing are the warriors I send into battle.

Tours, weekends, folk dance classes, club date bookings add to this arsenal; telephone calls, brochures, publicity, fliers, letters are powder to activate my war machines.

War!

Study war!

Daily life is my battle ground.

Peruse the shelves. Read more books. Study, learn, grow skilled in the fighting game. Though body cracks, finances fold, audience disappears, customers vanish, resources strain and drain to the breaking point, nevertheless, like Don Quixote, fight the windmills. Illusion or reality, who cares? War is war. I'm in the fight.

No person can fight my war. I am alone.

But I do have God on my side.

I see Armageddon up ahead. Forces of good and evil arrayed against each other. Good appears clothed in Survival and Excellence. Evil rears its head in countless Obstacles along the path. Marshal the arts! Gather weapons of business!

War begins today!

Who Knew Italian?

I came out of the womb. The doctor slapped me on the back. I started crying.

I realized only years later that I had wanted to enter the world "Italian style." Instead of crying, I should have shouted at the doctor: "Hey, whatta da fuck you doing? Hey, fucka you! Putta me back! Putta me backa righta now or I'll killa you! Bang, bang! I shoota you dead! Putta me back, you lousy fuck!"

That's what babies wants to say.

I should have said it.

But who knew Italian?

Positive Results of Getting Sick

I know best about my own health!

I know more about how to care of myself than doctors, health specialists, dietitians, mothers, vegetable eaters, and pill-popping vitamin believers.

Since I know my mind better than anyone else, why shouldn't I know my own body—a reflection of mind—better—than anyone else? After all, it is my body. I've lived in it day and night for years. Others may know about it from the outside but I know about it from the inside.

If I don't know myself, I am the only one who can find out. Others may have theories, ideas, beliefs, and convictions. Many even claim to "know" me better than I do. Let them suffer with their illusions. It is only important that I do not suffer from the same illusion. My job is to remember that it is I who ultimately knows what is right for my mind and body.

Sleep

Why go on vacation when I can go to sleep instead?

Sleep is a great medicine. And it's free!

On the Importance of Making Yourself Sick

Do I often make myself sick in order to protect myself from something worse? Yes. Sometimes "getting sick" is not as bad as the alternatives. This speaks to the "inner wisdom" of getting sick.

Why shouldn't my body need protection from my ideas? After all, it is a frail vehicle compared to the overwhelming force of an idea backed by spiritual power.

On Imagination

My run-away imagination is very strong.

Give it an idea, and it will expand it in hundreds of possible and impossible ways.

Such imagination is a strength. But I also need protection from its excesses. Thus the need for, and survival importance of, "calming mechanisms," such as self-created put-downs.

Although they often feel miserable, putting myself in second place protects me from the over-excitement and excessive stimuli my imagination feeds into my mind. Put downs protect me from the fire.

My job is always to find a balance, between the fiery ideas and stormy revelations of imagination, and the calming, wet- blanket of second place.

First Sparks of a New Life

A spiritual life is fine, and so is a mental one. But without my body neither is of much use. If my body is weak or sick, I'll concentrate mental energies on it and won't be able to focus on spiritual aspects of life. Working on the body, temple of the soul, is a spiritual exercise in itself.

After my post-Greek tour colds, coughs, sickness, and back ache, I decided it is worth spending mucho time taking care of the body.

Three hours a day. Back to the '50s.

Russian squats and Greek Tsamikos step practice. Then add jumps for the Tsamiko scissor step.

Running and calliyoga. Work to cleanse and strengthen my temple.

Hidden Power

Fears are signs of energy rising. By facing them, dealing with them, and finally incorporating them into your being, they become sources of tremendous strength.

Fear is a hidden avenue of inner power.

Thoughts About Alzheimers

Has Alzheimer been misunderstood? Perhaps people with Alzheimer's want to forget. They have simply become weary remembering all the miserable details of material and bodily survival in this world. They yearn to meditate upon the One. But how can they when their mind is cluttered up with so many details like shopping, paying bills, driving directions remembering children's names, and etc. Wouldn't it all be simpler if you stepped out of life with an excuse like "I can't remember anything." And to frame it all as a named disease like Alzheimer forces others not to say you're a burden. Rather it makes them sympathetic to your plight.

But is it a plight? Only on the material, worldly level. On the spiritual level, it may well be a door opening into long-term meditation on the One. After all, who has ever interviewed Alzheimer's patients? Who knows what they are really thinking? They always say they forget. Even if they do say something, we discount it by saying these are words from a "sick" person.

> Terror can overcome rage.
> But rage is an antidote to terror.
> Especially indignant rage.
> Defeat terror with indignant rage!

It is often a tremendous disappointment to realize that reality exists and I am part of it.

On Going for a Medical Check-Up

Should I go to the doctor for a check-up? Maybe.
But maybe I shouldn't.
After all, the doctor may tell me I am sick. I may end up believing him even if he is totally wrong. The wrong belief he instills in my mind will then send poisons into my body that will, in turn, create the very disease the "doctor ordered."

Yes, part of me is afraid to go to the doctor for a check-up. I am afraid I might believe him. I also am brazen enough to think: "What can the doctor know that I don't know already?" If I am the one who knows my mind best, I may also know my body best.

Many family members gathered at the Christmas dinner table.

They all said "Jimmy doesn't know best. The doctor does." They belileve that through internal examinations, diagnosis, and high-tech medical instruments, doctor's can find things I would never know or be able to find. They can make an early diagnosis of incipient cancers in my prostate, polyps in my intestines, catching sickness and disease in their early stages.

All this may well be true.

Perhaps I cannot know my body as well as the doctor.

But perhaps I can.

Aside from the aches in my muscles and joints, which I see as growing pains, I feel well. I have lots of experience with them. They have always been related to mental states. When my mind improves, these pains suddenly and miraculously disappear. If my mind created the pain, my mind can make it go away. Happily, I believe this despite dire predictions from doctors of what will happen to me if I don't get a check up.

Do I believe in my personal ability to cure myself, in the power of mind and spirit to not only create disease, but to cure it?

I do.

How about a medical check-up? Well, it wouldn't hurt. But I doubt it will help either. If I am in pain, then I am "inspired" to go to the doctor. But since I'm feeling okay, why bother?

Of course, I could get a check-up for preventive reasons. Again, going for such a reason can't hurt. But that is not enough incentive to do it.

How about those "morning wake-up pains" in my shoulders, neck, and knees, those a.m. mental creations? Doctors can't do anything about them anyway. So why go?

I like the challenge and adventure of learning to cure myself "on my own." I am searching to discover if my bottom-line beliefs are right. Does mind create and destroy the world? Can it create disease and destroy it? I am doing a self-cure experiment on myself to find out.

I believe yoga and running can cure me. When coupled with the medicinal powers of guitar playing, singing, dancing, writing, the dynamism of my own business, I have found a dynamite self-cure combination.

Most vitamins, minerals, supplements, and health foods are grown in my inner life. They come from the garden of mind, the artistic chamber of my soul.

What can the outside world offer me? Mucho tzuris.

Is there any way out of this dilemma?

Yes.

Squat steps: aiming for summer Russian tour of 2000. And Russian language.

Greek steps: aiming for Greek tour. Summer 2001. Greek language, too.

Tears of happiness! I've finally returned to my beloved dancing, languages, and tours.

Energy of the lower chakras as felt in cobra is down, dirty, and rich in dark nutrients wriggling in wet-brown humus soil.

Use it. Feel it. Send it to the upper regions.

Making the effort is my best medicine.

Extremes and the Limitless

Why do people go to extremes?
To discover limits.
Why discover limits?
To discover the limitless.
Where is the limitless?
Within.
When you discover the limitless within your self
Extremes become boring.

Then fade away.

Weight Training

Weight training is appreciating the beauty around you while carrying the burdens of life on your back.

Self-Appreciation?

A step into the New Land of Appreciation is not as easy as it looks. Not everyone wants to live there even though they might say they do. Too scary. What if you actually saw the world in all its magnificent, radiance, and glory. You probably couldn't take it. Too much. It might destroy preconceived notions and vested attitude of misery and hopelessness. Who can stand such a change? Better to retreat into lesser modes of anxiety, depression, or worries about the future. The walls you create protect you from that grand vision of glory, majesty, and magnificence of the radiance within.

This power within can burn away diseased cells. It can burn away those brain cells of limited vision which see only barriers in front of you. Limitless vision is too scary for most. This includes me. Oh sure, I may dream, think, and wish for such an apocalyptic vision. But when it comes, watch out! Too much! I might accept a glimpse, a whiff of infinity, but please leave me out of any permanent long-term vision. How could I continue my small life with it? How could I worry about bank accounts, relationships, marriage, life, or death? How could I focus on my miseries which give my mind something do by filling up empty moments passing through my head? Who wants those vacuums filled with radiance or glory? Not I. No, no! Give me Pathmark, ice cream, food supplements, bone damage, falling stocks, or warts on my hands.

I'll do almost anything to limit my vision.

Don't tell me people want to be happy. They just say that to make conversation. Of course, some might believe it until the possibility emerges. Then they run like crazy into the wilderness, inventing clumps of sickness, planting forests of new diseases, overturning dirt piles covers with leaches, or sawing down trees of ancient dreams and turning them into stumps. it! Take away this radiance! I can't stand it! Get rid of it. God, Radiance, Power, Divine, Pipsqueak, Buddha, Chin-Chang, Kung Fu, Chi Kong, Henry, or Gladys? Well, whatever you call it just get hin out of here! I want to keep my mind small. I want a limited world. I'm safe within walls of fear and worry. Shouting at ants crawling through my basement energizes me.

Don't take these pleasures away.

Obstacles

Lacking obstacles, you create them.
Obstacles are the flames of life.
They create sparks and ignite the struggle.
Conquering obstacles is not as important
As having them.

Success is the ability to live in excitement.

On Holding Yoga Postures

Movement breeds flexibility;
Holding builds strength.
Transfer the held yoga postures with their concomitant strength building to other areas of life.

Passion in Squats

There is passion in Russian dance squats, and Greek Tsamikos back-bents, too.
Passion in squats, back bends, and turns on one squatted leg.
Practice Russian dancing, and the Greek Tsamikos.

New Mother

Invent an image of mother encouraging me to be strong, dynamic, and wild.

"Yes, I love it, Jimmy boy! Go for it! Do it! I admire your power, strength, wildness, and dynamism! Jump into the abyss. Not only do I shiver and thrill at your daring, your bravery to take chances, but, just to show support and personal interest, I'm jumping with you!

"Yes, I'm joining you in the abyss not only to feel compassion and sympathy with you, but also because I'll enjoy it too. I want an adventure. It's not just you, you, you, but me, me, me, as well. I admire, respect, appreciate, and thrill to your love of adventure. I want to be go it. That's why I had you as a son.

"I'm your new mother. I'm here, not to clip your wings, but to fly with you!"

There is strength in emptiness.

On Setting Limits

My mind sets limits—150 push-ups, 150 squats, 150 sit ups—Then I work to reach my limits.

I set my own limits. I can adjust, increase, decrease, and change them.

If I set higher ones, will I fulfill them?

What does this mean for push-ups and other goals of life?

Teacher!

Become a teacher!

Ma and Pa will be proud. "You, a teacher! My son, the teacher!" Then they might say: "A guitar teacher, a folk dance teacher? Well, although he's a kindly person, he was always a bit off."

When I grew up the belief in education was a fundamental value. I believed in it.

My parents said, "Jimmy, once you get your teacher's license you can become a public school teacher and have financial security. Then you can be an artist or whatever you like. You'll have summers, holidays, and weekends off, too."

To me, this Bored of Education concept was the absolute wrong reason to be a teacher.

Become a teacher because you love study and learning. That's it.

Turning Point

If others ask me how I am or what did I do today and I give them the real answer, they might lose interest. They may fall asleep before my eyes as I talk about word origins, the history of sound changes in the name Carthage, or how the name Barcelona comes from Hamilcar Barca, the Carthagenian general who assembled an army of Spanish infantry and Numidian horsemen when planning the conquest of Italy; after he died, his son Hannibal, along with his army and elephants, defeated Rome at the battle of Cannae in 216 B.C.

If I tell others, they may not care. But so what? I love it. What great cracking sounds! Hamilcar! What, by the way, does the name mean? What about his second name, Barca? To me, these are great questions. Their answers are certainly worthy of pursuit, especially when someone asks me "How are you?" or "What did you do today?" It could start a great discussion. I might even find an answer to my questions. Worst case scenario, they may become bored. In that case, I'll keep flying my thoughts and pursue my answers alone.

In my mind, I fascinate myself. But outwardly, I rarely reveal these wild, weird, dynamic mental twists to others. Well, that's over. Others shall know. I'm going public as an "interesting person."

Mad Shoe Moments

What is a mad shoe moment?
Spirit descends,
Higher forces fill your mind with awesome power:
Wonder enlarges you,
Light shines from your eyes,
Drunk with spirit, you jump, run wild,
Dancing with ecstatic happiness,
Crazy for the divine madness that
Floods your being:
That is a Mad Shoe Moment.

Awful Feelings and the Smorgasbord of Creation

Awful feelings make me creative. They motivate me. I'll do anything to get rid of them. Often ex-pressing them is the only way out.

Psychoanalysis will never "cure" me. Even if it could, would I want to be cured? Evidently, unpleasant as they are, awful feelings are part of creativity's life's blood. Without them I might be dead. They feed me. Becoming aware of them is important. For that psychoanalysis is good. But getting rid of them is a completely different matter. Aside from being impossible, it is not even desirable. Well, it is possible to get rid of them: A frontal lobotomy will do it. But that is not the route I want to go.

Nausea, disgust, sorrow, anger, elation, disappointment, frustration, wonder, awe, they're all a necessary part of the cornucopia of creation. Indeed, they are "aw-ful" in the true etymological sense of the word: awe-filled.

How about body aches, pains, emptiness, fatigue, sleepiness, and the physical agonies that accompany daily life? They too are nourishing. Instead of trying to get rid of them, I might try having confidence in my misery! A new welcome mat for frustration, pain, mental anguish, back aches, arthritis, and the long list of human miseries that accompany existence. They are all food, nourishment for the creative mill.

The upward path of agony and ecstasy is the redemptive path. Unlike Marcus Aurelius and the Stoics, I do not want to simply endure suffering. But rather, like the mystics, I want to welcome it as a pathway to higher learning.

Syrtos and Seven-Eighths Time

I stopped the folk dance class to explain the musical structure of the Greek syrtos. I took a piece of paper and wrote down the seven-eighth's time signature and four musical measures of the dance. I pointed to the seven and said, "There are seven beats to a measure." Then I wrote down a dotted quarter note followed by two quarter notes. Then I explained how each note or, in this case "beat", was "attached" to a step. There are twelve steps—slow, quick, quick—or 1,2,3, 1,2, 1,2. Or right, left, right; left, right, left; right, left, right; left, right, left. That's the structure, and the way I think when I analyze, then teach, a dance. My students stood around listening. I'm not sure whether they were mesmerized, lost, or bored. Perhaps all three. Then Jeff pointed to the eight at the bottom of the time signature and asked: "What does that mean?" I explained that the eight referred to an eighth-note, and pointed out that each measure had seven eighth notes in it.

That's when I realized my students had no idea at all about the musical and theoretical structure of the dance. This was amazing to me. But, of course, why should they know? They have no training in this. I, on the other hand, have a lifetime of musical training. When I dance I always think in terms of musical measures. It's second nature.

It made me realize how much I have "kept hidden" from my dancers. Perhaps I should teach them theory. How, really, can you survive as a dancer without it?

Health Fascism.

Dictatorship of safety.
Health and safety as totalitarian tools.
You will wear a helmet. You will wear a seat belt. It's for your own good. If you don't do it, we'll arrest punish you. It's the law.

You cannot smoke. You should not smoke. It's wrong, evil, and bad for your health. It's not against the law yet. So instead we'll use the judicial and sue these mean tobacco companies into oblivion. We're doing it for you, to protect you from their evil ways and products. We don't worry about freedom. we don't even care that cigarettes are legal. Freedom is not as important as health—especially your health. But since you're too stupid to make the right choices, we'll make them for you. Besides, we can make lots of money shaking down these giant, dirty, death-by-smoke companies.

On Selfish Acts

I believe in selfish acts, the more selfish the better. Perform enough of them and soon you reach your true all-is-one home where the universal self resides. That is when you realize selfish acts are really selfless acts in disguise.

Mentally, include others when I do push-ups.
They are part of the Universal shoulder.

Fun Center Voice

The voice of Sylvan Woods in *Mad Shoe* is the same absurd voice that often pops out when I perform. It is my voice of the absurd, born of the miseries, pains, pleasures, joys, contradictions, paradoxes, ups and downs, vicissitudes of life. It contains the ridiculous, humor, and grace that protects and enhances me at parties, social events, and public functions. It has a hidden smile, sparkling eyes, the secret humor behind the concrete wall. It relaxes my students—the ones that get it—and it relaxes me. But, better than that, it puts me on the higher plane of freedom space.

Strange State

I'm making calls and promoting my tours. On the one hand, I'm functioning on a high level; on another, I hardly feel I'm doing anything at all. I neither feel bad or good about this. I'm in a middle state.

My motivation pillars have been cut out from under me. Nevertheless, without my pillars, I'm working just as hard as ever. Perhaps even harder. Yet it feels like I'm doing almost nothing. The public looks in: Jim Gold is working hard, functioning well, doing all the right things. He's on the road to success; he is a success. But when my inner world looks in, it says: What is Jim Gold doing? Hardly anything. As his body and mind move in many directions, his inner core is practically motionless. He feels neither up or down. Where is he, anyway? From a Zen Buddhist point of view, such an inner state sounds good. But Jim Gold is puzzled by how it feels. Actually, it doesn't "feel" at all. That's why it is so strange. He doesn't know what to make of it. He is both there and not there at the same time.

He is in a strange state. He is even writing about himself in the third person!

Triathelon Mode

Reading *New Leaf Journal* often reminds me of thoughts and approaches I have forgotten. One such quote is: "Happiness, even ecstasy, is based on total focus and concentration." Even though I wrote this, I keep forgetting it. If I benefit from my own words, others might benefit as well. Another reason to publish *New Leaf*.

Let's look at focus and concentration.

On this trip to Santa Fe, my schedule has been: Rise at 4:30 a.m., drink coffee, make entries in *New Leaf*'s "On My Own," section, then edit *New Leaf Journal 2*. This is followed by calliyoga.

I've been doing this yoga for one-and-a-half to two-hours! This is nothing new. Now I'd like to add a two hour routine to my life. Add an hour of running, or even two, on alternate days. I'm not sure how I would fit this into my busy Teaneck schedule. But I see how important it is. I want to put this return-to-Teaneck, triathalon approach into my life.

The triathalon athlete trains for three events: running a marathon, swimming two miles, and bicycling a hundred miles.

My triathalon would be: running (whatever number of miles, but based on one to two hours), calliyoga (which replaces swimming and bike riding), and folk dancing. That would make it a triathalon.

Training in this manner is a time-consuming top priority. In order to do it, I have to think retirement. This is a mental trick I am using to rationalize my desire to do this intense training. I would love to train in this manner. Such training is a good-in-itself.

How can I, an artist, spend so much time focusing on my body? How can I rationalize devoting so many hours on simply cultivating my physical form? Sure, I can see spending such large amounts of intense practice time on guitar, violin, writing, or such worthwhile pursuits as study or promoting my business. But to spend it "merely" on my body, to rationalize it through the search for ecstasy and fulfillment, seems so frivolous.

Is this a thinly disguised form of disdain for athletes, athletics, sports, and the body itself? Is it the puritan ethic in invisible form? Is it my family values of arts and intellect über alles which I have adopted?

No doubt, it is all of these. However, the time of their demise has come. I need to take a fresh look at athletics. I have always loved athletics and physical things. Body activity, physical movement, is my path to ecstasy and fulfillment. Witness my four-year-old, running-wild-on-the-lawn, followed by my love of baseball and basketball. For me, art, through the violin and music, and sport, always fed each other. What is folk dance and dance in general but a the blending of art with sport, beauty expressed through the body.

I search for a reason to do what I want to do anyway. I love the feelings that running, calliyoga, and my "new" triathalon schedule give me. Why not simply do it and shut up?

Visits

Mr. Death visited my mind. Is his visit just another scare in a long list of scares invented by my mind in order to dampen jumping joy?

Mr. Death promotes questions like: "Why bother?" and "What's the use?" I've heard these downer questions countless times before.

When Mr. Death visits my mind he creates rationalizations to give up, give in, and give out.

He is really just a bully, just another excuse.

Meanwhile exercise, food, and toilet care maintain the temple of the body. When the temple crumbles, spirit builds a new home.

The temple of body is a temporary residence.

Spirit is a permanent home.

Remember this.

Fervor creates motivation! Without it, deeds will not be done.

Look to My Mind

Instead of saying "My feet bother my mind," it is time to say, "My mind bothers my feet." Not only does it bother my feet, it creates their problem.

Instead of looking at my body as the source of my pains, look to my mind. Why is it bothering me?

I don't know. But at least I'm looking in the right place.

Caring for the Body

I have started my Anti-Ache Exercise Program. Once again, I must say, it works. This morning I woke up with hardly an ache. What did I do yesterday to deserve this?

Well, in a back-assed way, I must thank Dr. McNerney. He said I must do the leg stretches intensely, morning, afternoon, and evening, and before bed. To these I've added most of my other yoga stretches. Basically, he said, do the exercises or else! The way he put it was," Do them or I'll hit you over the head with a baseball bat." And this after I asked him, "How are my feet?" His answer: "They stink!" Well, he is not your basic touchy-feely kind of doctor. I walked out of his office quite depressed.

But no more. This morning I am up. It is because of Dr. McNerney. By stressing how important the exercises were, he promoted what I love doing anyway: namely, yogic stretching exercises. Only he put it in really stark terms: Do them or die! Do them or get hit over the head with a baseball bat. Then I added: Do them or you'll never dance again. . . or run, walk, hike, climb, or any of the active things I love doing.

So, Dr. McNerney is what I would call an angel in reverse. He gives the good news with a terrible delivery. Nevertheless, he does deliver.

Is exercising two to three hours a day extreme? Am I weird for wanting to put in so much time on "mere physical activity." What about so-called worthier things like art, culture, and intellect? Shouldn't my time be spent developing these? Isn't the body at best merely something to be maintained in the hope that you can ultimately, forget it as you move onto higher things? Can taking care of the body be a good in itself?

Great questions. I've always liked my exercises, the rush of positive feelings they bring, and the feeling of well-being I have after I do them. Wonderful, indeed.

But part of me feels guilty spending so much time at mere physical activity. This value system must stem from my childhood. Why this disdain for the body? Intellectually, I do not believe it. But evidently, emotionally I do.

Could taking care of the body become a spiritual path? Why not?

Caring for the Body Continues

Each day I follow the McNerney Anti-Arthritis Exercise Program, I get better. This morning I woke up with almost no aches and even walked up stairs "normally."

The heart of the McNerney program is doing the exercises four times a day. Actually, he said two: morning and evening. Then he said do them before and after you exercise. But I exercise every day. Plus, even on the rare days that I don't, the idea of four times a day is a good one. That means early morning, before lunch, late afternoon, and evening before bed. Or, when I exercise, that is, run, I do them early morning followed by a run, then do them again after the run, once more in the late (or middle) afternoon, and finally again at night before bed.

The "before bed" may be very good in itself. It puts the mind in an exercise, anti-arthritis mode. You fall asleep in this mode and wake up the next morning with healthy thoughts in your mind which, in turn, affect the body and make a smiling, wake-up walk.

Raging Infant!

I see myself at about three months old screaming helplessly as I lie on my back, my arms flailing in the air, my legs kicking like mad. And all to no avail. My mother will not come. And when she does, she still doesn't satisfy me. No one and nothing can satisfy me. I scream into the day, and cry into the night, I rage and kick. And all to no avail. Finally, my mother comes in and says, in her primitive body language, "Stop screaming!" My infant self hears it as "stop complaining," and worse: "Something is wrong with you for complaining, for wanting and needing; something is wrong with all your primitive wants and desires. Now, shut up! Be patient! You'll get your turn as soon as I'm through with your sister."

But my turn never comes. And when it does, it is too little and too late. By then, perhaps weeks or months later, I've already defended my screaming needy core by retreating into myself. I've put up the belly button walls, retreated behind the closed doors of my newly former room.

But I am left with feeling awful about myself. Disgust, rage, and terror. Part of me wants to kill! I hate, hate, hate! I'm screaming mad, and still nothing gets done. I can't stand the frustration so I protect myself by disappearing into the maw of my self-enclosed chamber, and covering myself over with a coat of disgust, nausea, and raging killer instincts, which want to pulverize and destroy these outer forces that have so hurt me by never giving me what I want.

I'm mad! This raging hornet's nest is ready to burst with sun-filled stingers and flaming darts. It is swirling, stinging, and angry, angry. Its surface form is "Do not touch me!" But deep behind the lines is the cry: "I can't stand it!" Deep behind that lurks the limp, whimpering refrain, "Who will love me? Who will love such a raging, screaming, noisy infant?"

What Is "Overwhelmed?"

If let loose, my wild self will flood the pages and flood the market. I will truly run wild. "Be nice, Jimmy boy," says my mother. "Stop screaming. Stop acting so wild! Calm down, be quiet. You'll hurt yourself. You'll get sick."

That's the "overwhelmed" feeling. If I run wild on the pages, I'll be bad. Ma does not recognize a bad boy. So restrain yourself. Do less. Write less. Pull yourself back.

The "overwhelmed" feeling puts a lid on wild energies, clamping down and closing off the true self.

Headache

Why do I have a headache this morning? Why am I at the borders of rage? Sure I had a couple of tour cancellations yesterday; I've been calling steadily since last Sunday; no checks have come in; business is very slow. Although all this is frustrating and annoying, I still don't think it is why I have the headache. That has more to do with the personal discoveries I am making. After all, I have stirred up a hornet's nest.

It is full of disappointments, and surrounded by protective walls that have hidden seething anger, screaming fury, and explosive rage. I raise my fist against my oppressors, those put-down queens who, for no other reason than ignorance, pushed me back into my belly button, stuffing my true self down the toilet of my throat, forcing me to gag, suffer, and whip myself into retreat, sending me back into my room, into the deepest corner of being, the land behind my belly.

Gag, suffer, and whip became so much of my inner life. Do not give it your all. Hold back, hold back, restrain, restrain, careful, careful, danger, danger. I've run much of life with the brakes on, lurching forward even as I skid into a rut. I hate, hate, hate it, but know no other way. If I ever break free, a strong intrapsychic hand pushes me back. Screams of exploding energy and joy struggle within me, grappling to leave my throat before a slap-down hand shoves them back. Down my throat they go, down my esophagus, into my stomach. I cannot win. As I release, I recoil. One hand gives, the other takes away. I go round in perpetual circles, never facing or recognizing the storms raging in my solar plexus center.

Will the opening of my solar energy center free me?

Stay tuned to find out.

Energy through Worries and Complaints

Why do people worry and complain?

Often it is their way of opening up their energy center, a subtle form of "turn-on." That is why they never want to be "cured" or have their problems solved. And if, for some reason, they get solved, they find new problems to worry or complain about.

Why?

People want to be in touch with the wonder and awesome beauty of their energy center. But the power generated there is so overwhelming, mysterious, and subtle they don't know how to handle it. Thus they create worries and complains to both connect with their center and keep it in check.

This energy center is, by nature, free, uncontrollable, and "uncomfortable." It is limitless, unbounded, and full of wild emotions. People hesitate to enter. Yet, like moths to the light, they are forever attracted to it.

Rest-oration at the Vulnerable Center

Resting between yoga exercises is where the restoration takes place.

"Rest" is in rest-ing and rest-oration.

Restoration comes from the Latin re-, again, plus staurare, to make strong.

We restore ourselves by eating in a restorante, or re- staurare-ant.

Meeting Noxious Influences

I sank yesterday.

After the collapse of my Tunisian tour I drifted into a business and financial depression. Suddenly, I saw no future in my tour business. It was over. This meant all my financial hopes had ended, that I would have to sell all my stocks to pay off my debt, and I would have to be satisfied with the small payments from my folk dance, booking, and even guitar lesson work. All my hopes crashed to the ground. Some of the old financial panic return. The "I will be old and dead soon," feeling; the "I'll be poverty stricken and end up in the gutter, a homeless, starving, neglected wretch."

These are not positive thoughts for a Sunday afternoon.

Now it is true that business stinks. But, on the other hand, "So what? What else is new?" Why am I being invaded by such negativity and hopelessness?

Am I allowing myself to be more open, to feel more of the hurts?

Or am I seeing that my fears, panics, and rages, my old reactions to business reversals and personal criticism as defensives walls set up to protect my soft, mushy, termite-ridden, sawdust strewn, vulnerable, beyond-the-belly-button, sensitive, loving core?

What a question. But, although I can do nothing about the objective fact that business stinks, I can always do something about my subjective attitude towards it.

Since I am now allowing myself access to a new vulnerable core place, I am more open and undefended. I'm letting noxious influences flow in. I want to take another look at them, see how they feel, taste, and smell. I want to get to know them.

Joyous Laugh!

When the true inner self is fully released, it comes out as a joyous laugh!

Keeping Hopes and Dreams Alive

My vital center was threatened, almost crushed, when it entered the dream-destructive, reality-driven territory of the outside world. To protect my treasure I hid it deep within myself.

Yet I dare dream in public.

If I dare, why give up on my Tunisian or Egyptian tours this year just because no one registered? They are still great tours. Why not simply run them again next year and see what happens? Great tours ever remain great tours. The sand storms, winds of change, and vicissitudes of business, do not change their nature.

Why be discouraged? Indeed, discouragement merely reflects a disbelief in future growth with its dynamic moves forward. It is the shadow form of the old neighborhood rock I once hide under.

Onwards, forwards, sidewards, and upwards!

Disappointment is a stimulant that creates resolve!

Obstacles to Goodness

Get to the point where you can thank others for yelling at you. See them as sent by a higher power to test your goodness. By combating such obstacles, you strengthen your resolve, and the knowledge of goodness within.

Rama

I got a call from Rama last night. He left a message on my answering machine. He wants to touch base, see how things are.

Rama represents my old life of idol worship. Basically, I worshiped him as The Knowledgeable Yogi, the Yoga Teacher of my

Dreams. Of course, he didn't see himself that way. But, for whatever reason, my old self needed to do that.

It no longer does.

When I meet him, again, I'll have to confront my old self. That is uncomfortable, even scary.

But, of course, that's probably why he called.

Joy is a State of Bliss in the country of Enlightenment.
But it is so hard getting through customs.

Free Afternoon

Reading the Torah in Hebrew and Hungarian is so much fun!

I thought it would be hard work to learn Hebrew and Hungarian, and that I should suffer and push in order to learn, self-improve, and grow. Instead I am simply loving it! It is so exciting to see the words in both languages dancing before me. I don't even know why, and frankly, I don't care. It simply is.

My only problem is accepting the fact I have this whole afternoon free! I can sit totally undisturbed in my living room and study!

Why can't I do this more often? Why not give myself the gift of a free afternoon—or even a totally free day! Once a week. Free to study, and nothing else.

Fun Radicals

Fun is so revolutionary!

It is a radical approach to life!

I once thought communists were tough. They were. But fun people are toughest of all! They're rebels who turn the world upside down. And they have a good laugh in the process!

Fun radicals run wild down the street tossing strawberries in the air and shouting "Olay!"

They are tomorrow's Luddites, dropping bananas in computer programs, filling bank accounts with Hungarian goulash, stuffing cash registers with broccoli and even cauliflower, and stepping on fresh-chewed sidewalk pieces of Wrigley spearmint gum.

Fun radicals wear mad shoes with no bottoms.

Snot River Symphony

I am sick of being sick. No yoga, movement, running, guitar, hardly any writing, no Hungarian, Hebrew, bible, improvements. No nothing. Call this a life? This cold has driven me back. I'm sick of sniffling and dripping snot onto everything I do. When will this faucet existence end?

The fact that I'm sick of it means I'm on the way up. Instead of entering my nose, my energy is now drifting into self-disgust. Self-disgust is related to self-loathing and, beneath that, to anger and total rage. Yes, after blowing my nose for days, these are all wonderful states. At least self-loathing can be creative. Anger and rage are high energy states. Anything seems better than sniffling, coughing, and retreating into the cocoon of chills and fear that my nose is turning into a stiff, frozen snot pipe.

I am writing the *Snot River Symphony*, the *Cough Cavern Suite*. I hate this kind of composition. Why did I go to the Juillard School of Music and Money Making in the first place? To write this kind of drivel? Instead of music I am creating mucous. Well, truth is, I never went to Juillard. In any case, compared to the low energy and creative value of *Cough Cavern Suite* and *Snot River Symphony*, self-loathing, disgust, anger, and rage are higher spiritual states.

Goodbye cold. Back to miracle schedule with a vengeance!

Mount Sinai and Heel Spur

I climbed Mount Sinai without a heel problem.

I run without a heel problem.

Only when I dance does a heel problem suggest itself. Folk dancing brings out my latent heel problem.

What is the relationship between my heel spur and folk dancing? Is it true that the movements in folk dancing are more intricate, intense, and uncontrollable than in my other sports? Or is there some base, psychological resistance reason involved?

I am hoping it is the latter.

Why?

Because then I can gain mastery over this pain, make it go away, control it. In the process, I would gain self-knowledge which, of course, would help alleviate the pain.

Is my heel pain hiding a greater pain? Do I create it in order to avoid facing a more refined but deadlier monster? Or is all this rumination merely rationalizations for a normal pain of life, or rather an abnormal normal life cycle pain?

I want to control my destiny. I hate being a victim. Somehow, if I cannot relate this heel spur to some mental condition, then I will fall victim to the inevitable forces of nature.

Once again the decision is so difficult to make. Am I my own victim? Or am I rationalizing reality? Am I creating my own pain, or is it being imposed on me "from the outside?" I want desperately to believe the former. But I lack confidence. The pain is too uncontrollable, sudden, and great.

Yet I could easily decide I have created it. If someone with authority told me that my heel spur is a mental condition, is caused by tension and nothing else, exactly the same as back pain, I'd be pleased. Dr. John Sarno says it is so. I would love to hear some definite statements from "experts" enhancing and supporting my hope that heel spur pain is my own mental creation. I even know that some experts do say it. But this morning, here in Budapest, I am a doubter.

Thus I am in a position where I can actually "chose" my why. I could pick the position of the experts who say heel spur pain is caused by tension; or I could follow the lines of the Dr. McNerney's and say that it is a physical deterioration, that I am on my way downhill, that it will only get worse in time, and, although I can alleviate the pain and even slow down my deterioration, the total decay and annihilation of my heel in particular and foot in general is inevitable and will sooner or later happen.

The former is the view of the medical mystics; the latter is the view of the medical materialists. I want to chose mysticism over materialism. So why don't I?

Could it all go back to my secret desire for pain as a stimulant? If

I accept the materialist view, then I have the promise of almost constant pain. . . and constant stimulation and motivation. I even create a constant goal: to get rid of my pain. This is a good long-term motivation. Goals are stimulants, too. Here is the plus side of victimhood, of constant pain or worry about pain.

And now we can also introduce worry as another aspect of pain. My worry that my body will fall apart, that my heel spur and instep pains will eventually force me to give up my beloved folk dancing and folk dance teaching career is another form of high worry and pain, and thus a constant stimulation and motivation to improve myself.

Thus fear and worry work together creating stimulation, motivation, and goals for my stimulation-seeking brain.

Leadership

I ran the seder with ease, confidence, and authority. My family loved it. I shone in their eyes. Compliments all around.

In a sense, it was similar to my Budapest and Prague tour. I also ran that with ease, confidence, and authority.

It is about leadership. Again I realized the leader's job is not to know everything or even to know a lot (although it can't hurt.) The leaders job is to lead. Period.

I'm good at it.

Master

Just as running tours and returning to Hungary (after eighteen years of tourism) seemed easy, peaceful, and fulfilling, so reading Jewish history again feels easy, peaceful, and fulfilling. Perhaps this will also be true for Hebrew, Torah, and Tannach study as well.

Studies in these new modes now seem easy. It's the "I've gone through this before" feeling. But with a difference. Somehow I'm now ready to return to these studies and travels, not as a beginner, but as a master!

A master? Did I say that? Me? Wow! How can I dare call myself a master?

But I can find no other word for it. I am simply comfortable in the mediums, be they travel, tour leading, or Jewish studies. To call myself master does not mean I know everything. I wouldn't want that even if it were possible. It would kill my sense of adventure, motivation, and love of learning. Perhaps master means "being comfortable in the medium." In terms of "telling others what to do," it means meeting lost souls in the forest, pointing out the route home, and saying "Go that way."

Thus, as a master I don't have to worry about imposing my views on others. That is not what a master does, anyway. A master is simply one who has mastered the material, and is comfortable in the medium. I have reached that point.

I have also become a master at leadership. It comes so easily and effortlessly now. Witness how I led the seder and my tour of Budapest and Prague. I hardly even try. I simply think I'm in charge, I'm master of this situation, and I take over. Again, no imposing of my views. Others want to be led. They want and need leadership as they wander and often lose themselves in the forest. They want a guru, someone to point out the path, and tell them "Go that way."

That's my job. In the process, I also supply them with that all-important ingredient, enthusiasm. I become their one-man cheering squad. I encourage them as they walk their path alone through the forest of self-discovery.

Threat Of Death!

I'm afraid of success. It may drain my life's blood, and destroy my passion. What can you hope for when you've reached the pinnacle? How depressing to stand there with nothing to do.

Success is a paradox, a full state filled with less, a plenitude of nothingness, a permanent resting place.

It is where the buck stops. . . dead!

Its incipient death threat trauma causes self-disgust, and can draw blood.

All problems have solutions.

All solutions create problems.
If there is no solution, then there is no problem.

Uncle Marty

Marty was my favorite uncle. I was so hurt when he told me I shouldn't go to France. "You must finish college before anything else," he said. He rejected my adventurous identity. After that, everything changed. I no longer trusted him. In his presence, I was on guard. I closed off to him. I now saw a rigid, hard-line, communist, narrow, tow-the-line, follow-the-forms, unartistic side of him I'd never known before. He was no longer the playful, fun-loving children's uncle who gave me shoulder rides. Ah, I couldn't wait for those shoulder rides, riding high up, holding on to his hair and neck! They were so much fun! Was this now the same person, the "real" him, the rigid orthodox man I'd have to face as a grown-up?

All Arguments Are Self-Arguments

All arguments are self-arguments. They are arguments with and within your own soul. The "outsider" with whom you argue is a prop set up to help you argue with yourself.

Arguments with "others" appear to be external, but actually, they are internal and with yourself.

Good Posture

I didn't stand up straight at the opening folk dance class on the GROW Weekend. Poor posture. I can't believe it. Me? After all that focus and posture work in front of the mirror? In spite of it, I took a step back into crouchhood.

Good posture is one of the highest values. And it is achievable.
1. Physically, it looks great.
2. Mentally, it feels wonderful.
3. Spiritually, it coordinates all my energies, uniting the chakra-linked spinal forces into a straight-line goal of strength. Good pos-

ture represents power in the present.

4. Pride in action. Pride is ego's recognition of the Power within.

Good posture is the king of positions. In physical form, it represents the proud power of God on earth.

On The Truth Of Illusions

I'm not willing to give up my illusions that easyily. After all, many of them may be good for me!

Illusions are dreams and hopes in disguise. They motivate and energize me. The "truth" of an illusion is found, not found in its illusory form but in the energy and motivational content within it.

Destroying one's illusions is not necessarily a wise idea.

In fact, the destruction of an illusion may well be an illusion itself.

But recognizing the beauty of an illusion, the truth of its energy and motivational content, is very wise indeed.

Expectation and More

I expect little from others. In fact, I often like to think I expect nothing from them.

However, expecting nothing from others is an expectation itself.

Thus, I have big expectations from others: I expect nothing from them. Not partial zero, half zero, but total zero. This is a negative expectation of perfection.

What is the difference between a demand and an expectation? A demand places others in control; an expectation places you in control.

How so?

A demand says, You'd better do this or else. Thus the other person can always refuse. However, an expectation comes from deep within you. You simply expect the audience or other person will act a certain way. Whether it is now or later, eventually they will come around to you.

One cannot live without the expectation, the hope, that on the road of curiosity, exploration, and adventure more is always coming. I practice expectation on violin and guitar. I expect to get better.

More is coming. I expand my tours and push for more tour customers. I expect business to grow, expand, and get better. More is coming.

My imagination creates the expectation that more is coming. I cannot live without it.

Worship through Work: My Highest Form of Service

I have God-given talents. They are mine. They are real. It is my duty to offer the fruits of my talents to others. This is my work, my means of worship.

My work is my worship. It is service to the Him within, the Hymn within, and the Him without.

When I admire monks living in seclusion on an island off the coast of Ethiopia, I am, in reality, admired adherence to my miracle schedule.

What do these Christian monks off the coast of Ethiopia do all day? They pray. They eat one meal a day, sleep four hours a night. They have no distractions. They devote their life fully to God.

Devoting my life to my miracle schedule is my way of devoting my life to God. The miracle schedule is similar to the monk's routine. It explains my attraction to a monk's life: Seclusion, retreat, and focus.

That's what I want to do.

Sure I have to eat, function, and survive in this world. But there is no need to live in it full time. Part time is fine. No time would be even better, but who's perfect? I still have a body. Nevertheless, to dwell in spirit, my spirit, is my goal and desire.

Roots

I see myself walking in the garden with my mother. I see a slow pointing index finger. Is it mine or hers? I do not know.

"Wait for my index finger, Mommy."

"Why?"

"Because it's slow."

"Naturally it's slow. It's more curious. It is your explorer finger pointing the way, visiting strange, mysterious places, touching the unknown. It has to move ahead slowly, hesitantly, carefully, cautiously. . . but very bravely. Ah, what a brave finger you have. What a brave and lovely son!"

He's the only person I know who strangled himself with a flashlight. He put the beam around his neck and squeezed.

World Trade Center

Shock, shock passed to sadness. This to anger at the Twin Tower collapse. New York and I have been attacked. The world has changed forever. A wake up call. There is before the "bombing" and after. Now is after. The American bear has awoken. We'll see what happens. But the solidarity, for now, is amazing. American solidarity and world solidarity.

I am amazed at how American I feel, how deeply and fundamentally I am an American. I've never defined myself that way before. I never realized its depth. Ask me who I am and I might answer, a man, a Jew, a former New Yorker, etc., and maybe parenthetically, an American.

But all that has changed. Now I feel a patriotism I've never felt before. My home, my beloved New York, the rock, has been attacked. I feel violated, saddened, and enraged. And it is so personal. There is no "they," "them," and "the others." The former "they, them," and "others" is now me. Yes, I want to fight back, help do whatever I can. But first I want to recognize this new depth of national patriotism, a deep sense of knowledge that I am so deeply and fundamentally an American. I have my deepest roots there. It is my home, and a grand part of me. This identity has always been so profound, so taken for granted, that I never saw it. But it has always been there. It took a national attack to make me realize it.

I love America!

I love the American flag!

I love the values American stands for! They are the healthiest, most uplifting values. They call on me, give me the opportunity to be and become my best.

But it took an attack on my beloved to make me realize it.

All former political squabbles and disagreements seen so trivial compared to this new sense of Americanism.

Americans have been complacent. We felt invulnerable. No more. That was the old world. Now is a new, "on your toes" game.

Let the military, secret service, FBI, CIA do their job and be their best! Toughness must reign. Naturally, alone with fairness, and love. But killing terrorists, the enemy, the evil, is part of fairness and love. Without the toughness to do the job, there will be no fairness and love. Only terror, fear, and the reign of dictators.

Thank Trauma!

Thank trauma. . . for creation itself!

If trauma forced me back into the room of my imagination, what did I find there? Imagination!

What is imagination but creation itself! The central, most important thing in my life. Something to live and love by.

Enthusiasm Is Adventure!

I'm blistering, smoldering, and a bit tongue-tied this morning. Can't escape the wahoos or the yahoos. New beginnings. Can't a worm ever have a moments peace?

Dithering and smithering among the ruins am I this morning. The hob has yet to bend the goblin, nor the exorcisms, freeing in their wake, not smite a bellies bottom. I can't seem to peck a word, either. A rocky, swallowy beginning on a pre-determined sea of fluff. Can a break-water stand upon a pillar? Can a sea gull fly over a Trade Center? What of pigeons or pebbles? Don't they have rights, too?

Given the bungling of such a morning, can a wallet ever seize the day?

Adventure is the game but I can't say a word about it. Add the adventure of finding customers. My essence is adventure.

My childhood trauma was not as much non-recognition as the clamping shut of enthusiasm! Enthusiasm comes from the Greek "in

God," in "theos.") It got no recognition from my Ma. "Calm down. Be quiet. Shut up. Go to your room to practice your violin." This shut down must have started around two-years old, maybe earlier, even a few days after birth. They kept happening. Clamp after clamp, lid after lid. Over and over, again and again they appeared. Soon I learned to push down my own excited. jumping mind by creating my own internal lids; I clamped down on public enthusiasm, shooed it away into my personal enthusiasm closet, the room of my imagination. There I kept it safe and warm and away from the noxious, evil, put-down, unappreciative, non-recognizing world around me.

How was enthusiasm expressed as a life force? Through adventure. Life as that adventure: Beneath its miseries, debts, mistakes, vicissitudes, horrors, and wonders, awe-filled and beautiful, fine and disgusting, all these, lies the essence: enthusiasm.

Turn every moment into an adventure. That is the quest and endless challenge.

Coffin lids over enthusiasm are everywhere. From a descending stock market, a collapsed World Trade Center, an anthrax attack, fears of disease, pestilence, and biological warfare; the frown forming on someone's face when you squeal with joy, the doubting killjoys that surround you at every step.

There are plenty of people and phantoms, both inner and outer, who will work to discourage and turn you away from your enthusiasm. Never giving in to their dire warnings, fear-filled alarms, and killjoy attitudes is your daily act of heroism. Watch out for those wet mops who hiss or cry: "Watch out, he's enjoying something! He's dangerous! Hurry, sit on that enthusiasm or it might spread!"

These warnings come not only from outsiders but often from within. Walls are everywhere. Tear them down. Go for the courageous. Become your own hero. Take charge. Embrace the realm of your true, enthusiastic, adventurous self!

Affirmations

Why would I need therapy?
To affirm what I already know!

But if I know it, why would I need it?

To convince myself that I know it.

But if I know I need it to convince myself that I know it, and I need it to affirm what I already know, and to convince myself that I know it, why indeed would I want it?

Good question.

Depression can be very restful.

Soaring

Death will come to me and all my loved ones.

Why do I think of it now?

It the newest form of morning lid placed over my expansion, over my guilty thoughts of happiness about my realization of freedom. It is awesome to realize I am free! I feel whipsawed with one foot standing in the new land of liberty while the other is still being dragged out of the sand pits of slavery.

Freedom soaring, flying out of my room and across the earth. This is new and frightening concepts for me to actually experience. I shield myself from its brilliance with downward thoughts of death.

It is frightening to die. But it is even more frightening to live. It is most frightening to soar.

What is the best choice? Spread my wings and soar!

Whiff of Rebirth

I am starting to wake up!

It began last night when, furious at letting my body fall apart, I returned from a Tuesday night folk dance class, and did an hour of yoga including 150 push-ups using the new breathing technique of 6 push-ups per inhalation and exhalation (one in, five out). For the first time in days, (weeks, two months?) I felt physically good again.

This morning, as I drank coffee and read about the ancient Syrian desert city of Palymra in Philip Hitti's History of the Arabs, I had my first travel inspiration in months. Here's what I wrote:

Goals
1. To stand in Palymra (visit Syria, study Arabic)
2. Visit Iran (study Farsi)
3. Visit Jordan (Petra, home of the ancient Nabateans)
4. Morocco, of course (or even Norway in Sept. or Oct.)
5. Yemen?
6. May Folk Festival in Sardinia
7. Egypt oasis tour
8. Norway, Sweden, and Iceland
9. Eastern Turkey

I begin my next travel journey. A whiff of rebirth.

What is Nestorian Christianity? I love the name. Research the spiritual glow of Nestor, whoever he is.

When you start forgetting, you need a new challenge.

Thoughts on the After-Life

I'm reading Jewish Views of the After Life by Simcha Paull Raphael.

Is there a big difference between our life on earth and the after life? Or is it simply an eternal continuum, an infinite voyage of the soul?

Life must be different lived without a body. It might be easier. No worries or cares about your health. I live in my mind, anyway. Mind is closely related to soul. Soul is eternal. So the difference between life on earth and the after life in a more rarefied atmosphere might not be that big after all.

If this is true, why worry about death? Although it is a drastic change, nevertheless, it is still "nothing permanent." I've been through lots of traumatic, drastic, earth-shattering changes before. Although losing my body would certainly be a new one, wouldn't it be "just another trauma" to deal with?

If the fear of death makes me think "Why bother doing anything since if all ends in death," and the soul does not disappear with the demise of the body, then why let the idea of death prevent me from forming new directions and goals? After all, if I don't finish my work in this life, I'll finish it in the next. Or the next. There is no end. In the long run, all directions and purposes are infinite. In the bigger picture, endings are an illusion. Why not live in the big picture?

More To Come

Where will I go after I die? According to early biblical Jewish tradition, I will return to my people, to my ancestors. I'll join Mom and Dad, my uncles and aunts, all the beloved (and unbeloved) people from my childhood and past.

A sad but happy view. Nothing is lost. I'll go home again. Very soothing. Actually, it is something to look forward to. According to the Jewish view, there is more to come even in the afterlife.

This afterlife idea is so restful, soothing, pleasant, and happy. There is nothing to fear. Death itself is just another family visit.

As for prophetic eschatology, on one level, I experience death and resurrection on a daily basis. Thus I am happy to say that eschatology and prophetic eschatology runs in my family.

Sin is not making your best effort.

Left Knee and Mother

On my first long run at the end of November I felt a slight pain in my left knee. On the following Folk Dance Weekend at Land of the Vikings this knee developed more pain. Soon it hurt so much I could hardly walk down the stairs.

I thought surely this annoyance will go away.

But it didn't. It hung in there, not getting worse, but not getting better either. Yet, within the confines of this pain, I was able to continue long runs, folk dance teaching, yoga, and callisthenics.

Yet the pain lingers.

Could it be a new repository for my fears? Isn't this a sign that "something else is wrong?" What about the idea that pain, disease, and sickness are teachers on the path of life, and once I learn their lessons pain will go away? I believe this philosophy. What does it say about my knee?

I don't know. Maybe I have to rethink fears in particular, and fear in general.

Could it be the fear the victory? I had a physical breakthrough. Finally, after months of delay, I am back to doing long runs! I did two hours at the end of November (and hurt my knee in the process.) Since then I've been doing one-and-one half to two hour runs every Sunday. These are major running victories. I am slowly getting back into running shape, finding new ways to combine my love of running with yoga and calliyoga. Ultimately, long runs are my biggest personal victory since the summer. Victory and success never sit easy on my shoulders. Nor on my knees. Perhaps I am "falling to my knees," humbling praying, and internally shouting, "No, no!" to my victories. Do I dare admit this publicly? No. I am too "cured." Thus I let my knee collapse privately. This may be psychobabble. But it may also be true. I would like to believe it is true. This would "explain" my continuing knee problem.

"You cannot be in shape, Jim Gold. You are too old. You are too weak. Someone your age should be in the hospital, in bed, collapsed and hidden in your room, cared for my your mother, or senior citizen nurses. You cannot be strong, dynamic, and bold. Don't you realize your travel business has collapsed? Look at your finances: a total mess. You'll be in debt for the rest of your life. Luckily, you are still a loser. That gives me a job. I can still take care of you.

"Yes, Jimmy boy, your mother is still talking to you from heaven. I haven't left your side. Oh no, not for a moment. You can never lose me. I will never leave you. Now I'm in your left knee. Notice the word "left." Yes, we were all left wingers. But you recently left (there's the word again!) the fold. You dared to strike out on your own and become, of all disgusting things, a right winger! How dare you have thoughts of your own! Now you are a capitalist slob, a renegade, betraying your mother's revolution. You slipped over to your father's side. Well, I won't have any of that. You're finished, Jimmy boy. Whether it be left or right you'll stay under my wing for the rest of your life! You cannot get away. Never, never, never! Dead or alive, I must have a function. Taking care of you is my function. I'll do it whether I'm in heaven or hell. You can't escape . . . ever!"

So speaks my mother in negative mode. I could say she is nice for trying to take care of me. I am also very aware of her existence deep in the subterranean caverns of my mind. Could she, and her dismal attitude towards my personal victories, be the prime cause of my continuing left knee pains?

I'd like to think so.

Since "I'd like to think so," why not think so? Why not start "thinking so" immediately? It will give me strength and a feeling of control over my problem.

Right or wrong here is besides the point. If I'd like to think so, I will think so! I'll move from vague to definite. In the process, my knee might get worse.

But it also might get better!

Garden of Eden

Why do we refuse to see the Garden of Eden?

Why do we jump at the chance to cover up our Vision of Paradise?

Is the pain too great?

If this is so, then the power of the Garden of Eden must be greater than the veiling power of pain.

Are Beauty more powerful than ugliness? Is love more powerful than hate? Are peace and serenity more powerful than war and inner turbulence?

Were we, as children, slapped so hard by the power of material reality that we learned to fear darkness more than light?

Going Public

The kids came in last night.

We sat on the floor playing guitar. I gave Zack my good Lo Prinzi guitar and Dave my good Diaz. I showed Zane how to play castanets. Then I took out my violin and tried improvising with all of them on Spanish and flamencan themes. From there I moved on to the gaida.

I tried teaching David the Macedonian melody Dimna Juda but it didn't quite work out. Then we tried Three Blind Mice. Zack strummed chords on the Lo Prinzi; Dave strummed chords on the Lo Prinzi; Zane bowed the open G and D string on my old Music and Art violin. I blasted forth on the gaida with a majestic, Bulgarian style Three Blind Mice! Three Sightles Rodents. Not bad. A potential winner.

Bernice and Jeannie sat on the sofa listening and admiring our sight and sound production.

Onwards and Upwards!

I read that Maimonides is a Jewish Aristotelian who believes in the dualism between body and soul. Since I am comfortable with this approach, perhaps I am a closet Aristotelian.

On to something else. What else? I want to write four pages of flowing jibberish. Let it roll. Whatever comes out is okay. Let mighty Hercules pullulate through my system. Let cataracts sound and the waters of protuberant Nile spill across the desert of my interior life. Flood and fecundate! That's the way to go! Other horses can sink into the sea.

It is not the intellectual or rational faculty that reflects the immortal soul, but the artistic and imaginative one. Let Maimonides roast in his Fostat seat. Let medieval Heliopolitan Egypt roast as well. Why am I focusing on all this roasting, anyway? I don't know. I just want to get the juices going, my roast flowing, my cooking up to par. This morning I have nothing say. So I must say it in flowery fashion to fulfill my four-pages a day quota. My commandment, my personal mitzvah.

Maimonides and most Jewish philosophers from the biblical to medieval periods say that to attain afterlife in the Garden of Eden and avoid negative penalties of divine retribution in the Hell of Gehenna, you must fulfill the mitzvahs.

What are mitzvahs? They are commandments.

Which commandments of mitzvahs should I fulfill? From whom do they come? From God Himself. But I hate to be told what to do. I hate being pushed around by superior forces or being lectured on good and evil even if the words come from God Himself! I like being my own boss. Sure, let God have His say. I don't mind if others participating in the game. But the last say, the final decision has to be mine. I'm in charge. I want the final word.

Nevertheless, I do follow commandments. But they are the ones I invent. This is true unless God is secretly working his magic through my brain, fooling me into thinking I create, make up my own life. After all, He could be a secret agent working behind the scenes, setting up my actions in such a way that I imagine I am inventing everything by myself. God knows I want independence so He gives it to me by creating my illusion of personal freedom. But the Lord knows all along where I am going or what I will do. He has predetermined it long in advance.

Anyway, whether the above is true or not, the main point is that I do follow commandments. I make up my own mitzvahs. Among them is writing four pages a day. When I follow this mitzvah I often end up in my own Garden of Eden, my personal paradise. If I do not follow my commandments, neglect my mitzvahs, I soon end up frustrated, depressed, sad, miserable, in a hell of my own choosing, a personal Gehenna beyond redemption.

Heaven and hell are right in front of me. They are part of my daily life. I don't even have to die before I reach them. Perhaps this is the modern version of biblical and medieval Jewish commands. Today we see things in terms of the present. Through much study, reading, and training in Buddhist philosophy tinged with dabs of Marxism, heaven and hell, are no longer far away, simmering and glimmering in a distant sun or shade. They are here-and-now. The communist state was supposed to create a paradise. Never mind that it turned out to be hell on earth. No one said humans are perfect. The practical application of communist philosophy, applied by power-hungry communists, certainly helped create a totalitarian prison, a contemporary gehenna. Nevertheless, the idea of having it all now, of reaching the future in the present, of experiencing eternity now, before you die, is a very modern idea.

I too am imbued with this attractive notion. But I'll not worship the communist state. I'll travel the path of inner vision by worshiping in my own in-room, personal temple created in the celestial artistic board governing the chambers of my mind.

How should I lead my life? Create then follow my personal mitzvahs.

Is there a common thread here? Yes. In order to be happy in this life or the next, one must perform mitzvahs. This Jewish tradition works. But it often has to be reinterpreted, readjusted, individually tailored to fit the multifaceted personalities that inhabit this modern age.

Dealing with the Success Trauma Syndrome

When I returned from my One Man Show Evening at Sons of Israel Temple in Leonia, I felt totally victorious. When Bernice asked me how it went, I said "Excellent!" She said you've never used that term before. I described the evening, how comfortable, easy, and wonderful it felt. I liked the format, the order of events. I began with forty-five minutes of beginner folk dancing. Then people sat down to eat. After they finished, I gathered them together for a community sing/concert. I opened with Irene Goodnight, then sang Oh Susannah Around the World and Tumbalalaika. Someone asked me what my footstool was for. I did my foot stool routine, then played Granados, Spanish Dance Number 5 on the classical guitar. The audience loved it. They sat in rapt attention, absolutely silent, listening with all three ears. I relaxed as I played and even lingered with succulent rubato on many of the notes. I followed Granados with a reading of Knorbert and the Kneecaps. That ended the concert section of the evening. I took a ten-minute break then concluded the event with half-hour of folk dancing.

I began the Leonia program with blasts from my gaida whose melodies alerted the audience when I was starting either my folk dancing teaching or concert. Loose and dynamic, in a wonderful and funny pushy way, I "ordered" the audience to rise, start dancing, and said this was "not a vacation." The artistic chamber of my private mind went public at every turn. I was an inner and outer success.

I woke up this morning with a headache.

No doubt this was due to the brain squeeze of success syndrome.

I want success but I also can't stand it. Total victory takes away my desire for more by giving me everything I want. As I win, I also lose. I get a universe filled with stars and sunlight; I lie happily in a womb of warmth, safety, and strength. But I also feel squeezed, straight-jacketed, bound, imprisoned within it. This conflict lies at the heart of my success trauma.

My quest is: How to live comfortably with the success feeling.

Run like a dancer. . . Dance like a runner.

Starting Over—Moving On

It started a few days ago when I played Alhambra six times in a row. I wondered if practicing in this intense, focused, repetitive manner would create a learning breakthrough? Sure enough, I did. By playing Alhambra six times in a row I reached another level of playing.

If this intense, focused method of practice works for guitar, will it work for yoga, calliyoga, running, and ultimately everything else I do?

I experimented. Next day, after my initial warm-ups, instead of doing fifty sets of three each push-ups, I did eighty! That makes three times eighty for a total of two-hundred-forty push ups. Most I've ever done in my life!

The following morning I added squats. Then in late afternoon, I did the scorpion, shoulder stand, leg over head, and lotus postures six time each! I ended up feeling very satisfied with myself.

Today I woke up aching. When I ran, I felt tight and tired. I analyzed my fatigue. It was caused by panic.

My breakthrough created panic.

Why? Recently, I have been afraid my body is getting old and verging on falling apart. I didn't have these fears a few months ago. Why now? I often frighten myself by my growth and expansion.

Best effort creates connection to the Higher Forces.

Resurrection of the Body

Is it possible for the body to grow in physical strength and flexibility as it gets older?

Is there physical resurrection?

Some ancient Jewish doctrines claim there will be resurrection of the body when the Messiah comes. Then all the "dry bones" of the field will leap together and be clothed with flesh.

But could such a thing happen in this physical life, in this here-and-now? In other words, can I get in better shape as I get older?

Life is full of suffering. But we also feel joy.
If you're Jewish, you can do both. You can enjoy complaining.
There's nothing like a hearty, "Oy, vey, vat a pain!"
My knees hurt when I did deep knee bends. Then I thought of a powerful healing image. When your knee, or any other part of your body hurts, picture an open gateway. Then visualize hot healing blood pouring into your painful area.

I tried it. It worked. Amazing is the healing power of mind.

The Revolutionary As Hero

Slow guitar playing is revolutionary!

To paraphrase Boris Pasternak: In times of great speed, the true revolutionary goes slow.

The revolutionary dares to try something new, be different, go down a new path, buck the establishment. It's just that now, politically, former communist, leftist, and civil rights thinkers are no longer revolutionary. They are part of the establishment.

But the true revolutionaries to me were always artists. Beethoven was the ultimate revolutionary. The artist, living in his garret, fighting for his personal cause, the expression of his artistic vision. He is my hero, my revolutionary.

When in doubt, go with the original idea.

Thinking About It

Thinking about something is doing something about it.

Thinking, imagining, is often followed by a deed. But the first step is always thinking.

The way to fight terrorism and evil is to absolutely not tolerate it. Squash it immediately and in place. Stop the evil and terror in its tracks. It only get worse if you don't.

Jealousy and Envy

In Greenwich Village days I was haunted by jealously and envy.

Communism and most of left wing politics is based on envy. This is the milieu I grew up in.

But I was never jealous of my classical music heros. They were gods, too distant to ever be touched. Jealousy and envy were reserved for people I could reach. They were mirrors of unfulfilled ambition and potential. Rather than see them as a source of inspiration, I turned on them, becaming jealous and envious of their talents and accomplishments. It was psychologically easier that way.

Jealousy and envy is at the heart of communism, socialism, and left leaning politics.

But I am now slowly adopting the entrepreneurial attitude of a capitalist. Glory to the individual! I love the person who tries! Making your best effort brings glory! The hell with jealousy, envy, communism, and left wing politics. I'vegiven up on "workers of the world unite!" Let them work instead.

Taking My First Political Steps

I can't stop reading and thinking about Israel, the Middle East, and its politics. I am passionate about it, and the love of Israel.

Will I now be able to talk about politics without getting tongue-tied with the usual, old neighborhood, anger and frustration?

Where does this frustration come from? My past, of course. Who would ever listen to me? What chance did I, or my father, have against my mother and her family communists? My father was the open minded, the only "liberal" in the old sense of the world who considered opposing views. He questioned the ideologues in my family, dared to doubt the moral superiority of communism. He even doubted that Stalin's Soviet Union was the paradise all my left-wing family and friends believed in. He even dared to question the doctrines of Karl Marx.

What was the result of his humanitarian, liberal (old sense), and heart-felt questioning? He was called "stupid," by the rest of my family. Naive and dumb. His questions cast away with a flick of the hand. He was irrelevant at best, a traitor to the cause at worse. Humiliated, laughed at, scorned. Indeed, independent thinking and open-mindedness was out of the question. Only stupid people tried that. The communist line was hard, definite, clear, undeviating, and true. It contained the Absolute Truth. Anyone questioning it was an idiot or a traitor.

Growing up in the suppressed atmosphere, seeing how political open mindedness was treated caused me retreat into the refuge of violin playing with its clear notes. Who would question that? All the notes were on the page. I could possibility become master of that realm. The land of music was my kingdom. No communists, Stalin, or Marxist doctrine here.

No wonder I presently quake in frustration, and lip-biting rage when political discussions come up. I have an ancient trauma on my shoulders.

Can love of Israel added to loving the strength, passion, and belief in my own views carry me through a political discussion? Can I stand up in public for my political beliefs?

Dare I even have them? Political beliefs used to be for smart people. I was not smart. "You're an artist, a musician. Your mind is in mush land, a fantasy realm filled with dreaming, waa-waas and goo-goos. We're not interested in your views. Go back to your room. Practice the violin, and shut up. When we ask you to come out, you can play violin for us. We'll smile, admire your efforts, pat you on the head like Lucky our dog, and tell you to heel! And you will!"

Am I now at a new "talk politics" stage?

Just asking the question means I am entering the new land.

I am learning to take my first steps.

Politics, Passion, and History

I have never been able to make the connection between passion and history. Thus it has remained a "useless" intellectual exercise. And yet, I have always been interested in history. I have been afraid to love it because love requires passion. I fear passion in history because it is connected to my secret and long suppressed passion for politics. True, my interest in history has also been expressed through the tour business. But my true passion, the one that touches manly and indignant rage, the passionate hatred of injustice, is in politics.

History, politics, and passion are connected. I have not, until now, consciously made the connection.

Studying history for my tour business is still an intellectual exercise and thus a step away. Knowledge of history is not vital for survival in a foreign country. Language is. Thus my passion has gone into studying the languages.

Politics, passion, and history. Going public with my ideas. I am leaning over the abyss. Daring and dangerous. Should I jump?

Self-Doubt and Confidence Are Partners In The Quest

The road of courage is strewn with doubts.

Self-doubt is simply part of the growth process. Since the future path is always unknown you can't help doubt yourself along the way. Traveling in the land of the unknown, am I going in the right direction is a constant question.

What is courage without self-doubt. How can you develop it without facing, confronting, conquering obstacles along the path. One must walk through fire in order to feel the heat.

Everything is going well this morning. Even my guitar playing has broken through. Yet I'm feeling low. Is it because I'm Jewish?

Giving Myself the Gift Schedule

During the Land of the Viking's Weekend I spoke with Aaron Kirshenbaum. He is training for a triathelon. He inspired me to make a new commitment to train!

Two hours a day of training. It's okay to allow myself this gift. Just as I gave myself the gift of writing two hours a day, so I can give myself the gift of two hours a day of training with yoga, calliyoga, and running.

Money and Its Brethren

Starting Over Financially

Twenty-five years ago I decided that, since I was smart and could make a living in the impossible field of music, I could ease and appease my financial worries by using my smarts to learn about money. From there I would slowly move on to being rich, and eventually become a millionaire.

I read *How To Get Rich Through Debt.*

Soon after I started my stock market and tour career.

This morning I awoke with the fixed at total realization that both careers are financial failures. Hard to admit. However, there is one financial venture I was successful at: building my debt.

Having and growing my debt was exciting for awhile. As long as I knew I could easily pay it off. My debt to asset ration was always about four to one. Plus I believed, "knew," nay expected to pay off the debts after one or two successful tours.

These thoughts took place at the beginning of my tour career.

My stock market ventures were a fascinating and fun sideline. At first my stocks rose. They descended slightly when I bought in the speculative Denver penny stock market. Even so, they remained four times my debt. Plus it was the beginning of an exciting financial and entrepreneurial learning adventure

Three years ago my stocks crashed. In a two month period they went to one-third of their value. After several months of panic, I got used to my lowered financial security and level. Plus, I still had hope my tours would pay off not only my debts but would even eventually make me rich.

Last February expectations for my Tunisian tour totally flopped. Numbers went from fifteen people last April to one this year. Sadly, I realized my tour business was over in the old making lots of money sense of the word. Plus, I came the understanding that tour monies would not pay off my debts.

In May, after returning from the Budapest-Prague tour—a mild success with ten people—my Gulf Canada Oil company, of which I owned 6000 shares, was bought out by Conoco. Suddenly, after four years of the doldrums, my stock market portfolio rose. I was back in stock market business.

I opened my own on-line Fidelity Trading Account. I made some good trades with my broker, Joel. Within a month, my portfolio doubled. I got excited. My hopes went up. Was I developing a new skill? Had therapy given me the mental ability to make up my own mind, take a chance, to buy and sell on my own? Could I do it all without Joel's advice (which cost and lost me lots of money.) Could I make money on my own trading in the stock market? Maybe.

I gave it a try.

By August my portfolio had almost tripled! I thought, at this rate, by December I'd have, or aim for, one-hundred thousand dollars. Then I would sell half, pay off debts, and move on from there.

At the end of August my stocks crashed. After September 11th they went down even further. I thought, here is a buying opportunity that comes once in a lifetime. I borrowed three- thousand dollars, put it into my trading account, and bought more stocks. Soon they started to go up. By the end of November I had almost doubled the level of my account. Again hopes rose. I took out books from the library on stock market trading.

In the middle of December the market crashed again. My portfolio went in half.

The result of all this was (is) when I awoke this morning I decided it may be time to give up on the stock market. After all the work, time, effort, hopes, and dreams I have put in, it still goes ultimately up and down and gets me nowhere. This coupled with the fact I now have to pay off debts with paltry folk dancing, bookings, guitar lessons, weekends earnings. It will take years (if not my entire life) to pay off this debt through such earnings. This puts me in a most uncomfortable place. It is actually painful. I don't like it.

So I have to rethink my life and money. Since my stocks may never rise high enough to pay off my debt, perhaps I should think about selling all of them off! True, I would have no assets in the market; but I would also have no debt.

This would really be Starting Over. Financially, I would end up exactly where I started off when I got married: with no money. Oh sure, I now own a house. That's an asset. Plus I have lots of confidence in myself. That's my best asset.

Financially, I am at new point: Starting Over.

Making Money Through My Art

Enron just got delisted. Another stock I own turned to shit.

I'm constantly getting battered by the market. I have no luck or skill in it. I only seem to lose money.

Am I being hit over the head to teach me that my skill in not in the market? I should get out of it once and for all.

I am an artist. Period. The stock market is not a place for me. I only make money when I work.

Thus my money should only go into supporting my artistic (and business) habits. This is the way I started out twenty-five years ago. I wanted to learn about investing (in the market) so I could eventually be financially free to follow and support my artistic desires. Well, I've done that.

It be ironic to discover that fulfilling my artistic desires is the best and only way for me to make money!

If this is true, (and I hope it isn't) then I should get out of the market. A partial solution might be to get out of the market partly... or mostly. But I hate half-way solutions. I go for the apocalypse. If I'm going to make a mistake, I'd like to make a big one, a significant error, so that, deep down, I really feel it! Mediocre success or failure just doesn't seem to do much for me.

Are the years I've spent in the market a learning blunder? Have I been simply treading water for the last twenty-five years, waiting until I got enough confidence in my art to find security and make a living in it?

Good questions, indeed.

My desire to acquire money and eventually become a millionaire phase was similar to my early desire to become a physicist.

After graduating high school I wanted to become a physicist so I this knowledge, I could do what I really liked, namely become an artist.

I always wanted to be one. But I didn't have the confidence back then.

Then, post-forty, I decided to become rich so that I could become an artist and not worry about money. Certainly, the past twenty-five year trip was a financial failure. But in every other way it was a success. I now have the confidence to be me, the confidence to be an artist!

Was it worth it? Yes. I can now stand up straight and proud and be what I really am. Free at last!

I am an artist! Yes!

What price can you put on such glory? Can you even put a price on it? Absolutely not. Glory is priceless.

That is my achievement. Actually, money, on the deepest level, is besides the point. The money is a part of the road to adventure, the turbulent, glorious road into the self.

What is my career? I don't have one. I only want to be an artist, a creator. Does the Creator have a career? I want to line myself up with His Higher Forces, work together with Him on all levels, at all times, in every way.

I Am My Only Guide

Last month I decided to focus on my business and forget about the stock market.

The problem is I can't forget.

I want at least one winner.

I have Vanguard. . . and Cirrus Logic.

Suppose, I am right about the path I've chosen. Though it is strewn with rocks and straddled by thorns, what else can I do but walk it?

There may be experts on this path but there are no guides.

I am my only guide.

Financially, I have led myself into the thicket.

Now let's see if and how I can get out of it.

"If" is fraught with fears; it contains the possibility of not only staying in the thicket, but moving even further into its entrapment. It points to lack of confidence, self-doubt, and second guessing.

"How" is practical and optimistic; it points to patience and steady competent work. It means I am on my way out.

I am on the road of How. But I travel with many cloudy residues of "if" over my head.

My biggest challenge is: Forget "if." Focus on "How?"

Arrogance Is Ignorance Misspelled

My relationship with money is ironical. The most important thing I want from money is not to think about it. Instead, I spend most of my time thinking of it.

I decided to enter the stock market because I thought: I am a smart person. If I spent ten percent of my time learning how money works, I will soon become a rich and secure. Then I can live as an artist without financial worries.

Due to my incredible intelligence and ability to accomplish whatever I desire, I would soon become a millionaire. This is a foregone conclusion. After all, I succeeded in making a living as a guitarist, an almost impossible task. If I can fulfill such a dream, why can't I succeed in the much simpler task of becoming rich? All I had to do was learn how to play the stock market. I didn't want incredible wealth. Who needed billions? Millions would do. I'd een settle for one million.

I have an amazing imagination. It even boggles my own imagination. The only thing more profound than my financial imagination was the profundity of my financial ignorance. Or was it arrogance?

Ignorance led to arrogance.

Arrogance is ignorance misspelled.

He Wore A Suit

I have no talent for the stock market.

Is this a failure or an awakening?

A real man makes money. The more real he is, the more money he makes. The model of malehood is the business executive. He is buttoned-down and tight-lipped, in total control, unflappable, unbeatable, tough, can "take it," never admits defeat. And he wears a suit, white shirt, and tie. A respected upstanding member of the community.

That was my financial model for twenty years. Naturally, the executive was a whiz with money and investment "skills" like borrowing and "handling debt." He could "take it" when and if the stock market collapsed and his stock investments fell in half or further.

And he wore a suit.

How long I chased this illusion which isn't me.

In accepting my lack of talent in finance I see a tiny light flickering. Seeds of inner peace are growing inside me. What a relief! Finally, I can give up the stock market, get off the financial torture wrack, and return to the artist that I am.

I will return with a deeper appreciation of my true talents and gifts. I'll not waste more time trying to be the financial giant I am not.

I can support myself financially—even as an artist. Before I entered the stock market, and decided to learn all about investment, debt, money, and borrowing, I not only supported myself but even build a savings account. All this was before I "decided to get rich." Finances then, although precarious, were simple and steady. Now I shall return to that former model. Belief in the magic stock market, has been utterly destroyed.

There are benefits from this destruction. But I won't go into them I want to recover from this blow to my ego.

Fun Is Your Birthright

My attitude towards money is a threat to the American establishment, capitalism, and the puritanical ethic.

I do not believe you should earn a living by the sweat of your brow.

I believe you should earn it through the fun of your brow, by playing with your eyeballs, by throwing your sweat up in the air, then taking a sweet bath in it.

Yes, I believe in fun! That's it. Everything else is postscript and footnote. This goes for earning a living and making money, too.

The only thing you have to "earn" in this world is fun. Actually, you don't even have to earn because it is your birthright. Rather, you have to discover it, become aware that, in its archetypical form of joy, it is your center and essence.

Buddha would have supported this fun idea. Except he called it joy. In order to find it, you have to "lighten up." That's why he called it "enlightenment."

Am I Mr. Fun?
Am I Mr. Fun?
Isn't Mr. Fun a frivolous title? What about my serious side?
Do I have a serious side?
Can "serious" be fun?
Why not?
Perhaps my serious side is my fun side, and vice versa.

Money and Running Wild on the Lawn

In my mental closet hides the "money is fun" idea.

Fun? Mad shoe, running-wild-on-the-lawn fun? How can I look at money, which is so serious and fraught with peril, as mere fun?

What will people say? What will mother say? You are childish, stupid, ridiculous, unserious, a mere child. Grown-ups take money seriously. It is not a plaything. Go back to your toys and shut up.

Growing up with this attitude towards money, and having it confirmed by all those around me, how can I possibly admit that I would like to have fun with it? How can I dare think such thoughts? It is a sacrilege. America thrives on money; people love money. It is the love affair par excellence. And I blaspheme by saying that playing with it, even earning it, is just fun. What happened to sweat, weight, and heaviness? Money is America's religion. What happened to mine?

Thus it is the height of rebellion and arrogance to look at money as a mere plaything. Father would be angry. He worked so hard to get it, slaved away at his principalship, trudged tired and hungry up the hill every weekday evening after a long, tiring day of work. He slaved away to support us. He suffered for our family, and for me! And here I take his sacred struggle to earn a living, and toss it away by saying his sweat money was a mere plaything, a toy, something to have fun with.

It is not right. Money does not come easy. Only a selfish child who likes and needs to be cared for would see it any other way.

But evidently, I am that child. I like to run wild on the lawn throwing money up in the air, playing with it, watching the wind carry it in all directions.

Well, so be it. Dare to be me.

The Miracle of Money

If business is going to be a miracle, and since so much of business is about money, then everything concerning money has to be a miracle.

Money is also a miracle.

What about filthy lucre? Now there's a voice from the medieval church, my mother, and the communist party. It certainly fits the communist agenda.

All the dirty, disgusting, oppressive capitalists had money. The proletariat, on the other hand, was clean, pure, and penniless. Indeed, the idea of filthy lucre comes straight out of my communist past with perhaps a little medieval church thrown in. Add a bit of apocalyptic Judaism, too.

My historic prejudice against money runs deep. To see it and business as a miracle is a personal expansion of premier order.

I am at the border of a new career: Stock trader.

Is my personality right for this? Can I succeed?

Success is measured in terms of money. How much I make will determine how successful I am. My feelings or what I learn from the market has little to nothing to do with successful trading.

Can I make money trading? Certainly, it is fun. But it is not much fun to lose.

In order to have fun, I have to win more often than not. If I only lose, I will not have fun, and that will be the end of my stock market trading career.

How can I win?

The Trading Art

The trading art fits me psychologically. That's why I love bargaining and buying in the souk, and its counterpart, bargaining and selling at my boutique. It's is just so much fun to stand there, talk to customers while you banter, bargain, and trade with them.

Notice the words "trading art." Trading is an art.

Is there a place for artists in the stock market?

Does the artistic temperament "fit" it? Does it apply to the art of trading? Is trading really an art?

Well, why not?

If I see money as stuffy and "responsible," then, of course, art and fun have little to nothing to do with it. If I see it as exciting, then money can be a field for an artist, and even an expression of the artistic temperament. Whether knowing this will help me succeed, I do not know. But at least on the most fundamental artistic fun level, it feels right.

A Time To Buy, A Time To Sell

When I get excited and optimistic about the profits of my rising stock, it is time to sell.

When I get down, sad, depressed, and pessimistic about the descent of my stock, it is time to buy.

This is an emotional truth, not a stock market truth.

But I can't predict the movements of the market. I can only know my feelings. Therefore, the "time to buy or sell" is only true on a personal level. It has little to do with the direction of stocks.

Making Money Is Fun!

Making money is fun! And this whether I earn it through teaching, touring, weekends, concerts, book sales, boutique items, and the stock market. Actually, it doesn't matter how I earn it. All I have to do is acknowledge how much fun it is to make it.

I've just done that.

Then why not make my summer project figuring out how to make even more money? Hey, I like it.

What will motivate me to publish *New Leaf Journal*? Selling it, of course. Seeing money roll in from the sales.

Should I record my songs, stories, and classic guitar pieces? Why bother going to all the trouble? Money. I can make money by selling the tapes, cassettes, and CDs.

What about running tours, weekends, or teaching folk dancing?

Why bother? I can make money from them.

What an excellent motivator is the hope and possibility of making money.

For my material needs I need little money. But for my fun needs, I need an infinite amount. Money is a quantitative measurement and representation of "more." I always want more. More, more, more: More study, more running, more learning, more concerts, money, higher stocks. Wanting more of everything and anything goes on forever. Wanting, wanting, wanting means I am alive!

But how about the idea that I want money not to relieve myself from fear, pressure, and worry. Some day, if I get enough of it, I can stop worrying and have more time for art.

This will not happen. Why? Because I have already stopped worrying. Worry and fear have little to no place in my financial life. And this is true, even though I have little money and big debts.

However, I am now onto a new adventure: Making money through the ventures I perform, through the art forms and organization skills I have developed over the years.

Making money has become a good-in-itself. Why? It has become the symbol of fun!

Playing in the money play pen, with lovely lucre is what I want. If I want it, do it.

Three Approaches To The Stock Market

I am like a child chasing stocks as they rise: "Oh, dear Triquint and lovely Cisco, come back, come back. Please come back to me. Do not leave me behind. Do no abandon me."

Didn't I promise I would never chase a stock, that I would bravely buy them when they went down and sell them when they went up? Of course I did. But was it a wise promise? Probably. Or rather, who knows? In the stock market, the answer is: No one. There are no signs from heaven commanding one to buy or sell. That's the tricky part. I start to panic that I will lose the stock before it runs away, hits new highs every day. Then I jump in and buy it. So often I end up buying it at the top. Right away it starts to descend. Look at my first purchase of Cisco Systems. After waiting four years, I bought it at eighty. The top. It slid from there down to thirteen. It also happened with Sensar Corporation. I bought that one also at eighty. Since it was a shit company, it slide to twenty five cents. So much for the twin nemesis of chasing a stock. Panic of loss and buying at the top. Of the former, at least I have "control." I can "decide" not to panic. Easier said than done, but possible nonetheless. As for the latter, since I can never know where or how far a stock is heading, I cannot know whether I am buying at the top or not. That one is for the gods to decide.

After all this blather, what should I do?

Here are some choices:

1. I can sit on the sidelines and do nothing; simply watch the stock, and wait in witness mode. I'll call it practicing witness mode.

2. I can take a small position in the stock. Say buy fifty shares. This softens the hard edges of either/or, and to-have-or-not-to=have. It makes it "easier" to wait. I'll call it taking a small position.

3. I can dive into the terror. I can look straight into my panic, abandonment, fear of loss, fear of being left behind. This is the psychological approach to the stock market. I'll call it the feeling awareness approach. Indeed, this one is new. Discovering it is exactly why I write.

Truth is, there are always other stocks, always ones that are low. I don't have to get attached to a particular stock; I don't have to "fall in love" with Triquint or Cisco just because finally they are going up. Certainly, my love for them is fickle. It is simply based on the vicissitudes of their direction: go up and I love them; go down and I hate them. There is no rock bottom solidity in this approach.

Indeed, the love feeling is lovely. It is romantic to love. And this whether a woman or a stock. The fear of loss makes a woman "attractive" just as the fear of stock loss makes a stock "attractive." This is indeed some shit way to buy a stock.

Do I want to live my stock market life in fear? Do I want feelings of panic, loss, and abandonment to enter into my decisions? No. But I am not a robot. Fortunately, or unfortunately, I have these feelings. They blow me about too and fro. Only awareness of their power can soften their effect on me.

Well, I am aware of them. So. . . .

What should I do about Triquint and Cisco? Which of the three "solutions" to my problem should I choose?

To reiterate: The big three are:

1. Practicing witness mode. This is the yoga meditative approach.
2. Practicing taking a small position. This is the compromise approach.
3. Feeling awareness. This is the psychological approach.

Actually, the practice of witness mode and feeling aware go together. As I sit on the sidelines and watch, I am witnessing my feelings.

Thus I have whittled the approaches down to two:

1. The compromise position of taking a small position.
2. The witness awareness mode of watching my feelings.

I still don't know which is best or what to do. But I have whittled my choices down to two.

My Mistake

My mistake in the stock market was to "go for broke." I margined myself to the hilt. This left no room to buy the great bargains that are appearing now as the fine companies I own descend into the shit price range. All I can do is watch while these delicious bargains get greater and greater. I feel helpless.

Helpless is no way to be free.

"Going for broke," leaving nothing on the side for those special days when the market falls apart, is not a good way to go. I margined to the hilt when the stocks were high, then panicked believing they would go even higher and I would be left out. So I bought more. Typical, of course. But still no good.

I did not limit myself. Thus did I fall out of freedom into slavery.

That was my mistake.

What can I do to right it? Sell half my stocks? Perhaps. It's painful, but it may be the best way to learn how to limit myself.

Shouldn't I suffer the consequences of my mistake? The idea here is not to punish myself but rather to learn in the process.

Playing Well

Yesterday, after talking to Charles Lee Booth, a Fidelity broker in Salt Lake City, Utah, I charged to the library and took out six books on trading, options, and the stock market.

The first one I open was called *Trading For A Living*, by Dr. Alexander Elder. He originally from the Soviet Union. He escaped by jumping ship in Africa, running to the U.S. embassy for asylum, and finally arriving in the United States with only summer clothes on and $25 in his pocket. What a story!

But what he says is even better. After reading Engel's *How To Buy Stocks* and telling how the book changed his life, he says, "I had known nothing about the stock market, and the idea of making money by thinking gripped me."

Elder's book has a section called "After The Trade." He says to keep a trading notebook.

Should I deep a trading notebook?

This question asks: How serious do I want to be? How much time and effort do I actually want to put into trading?

Good questions.

The Stock Market Popped.

It hit bottom, then turned around.

I also hit bottom, then turned around. Evidently, my feelings are intimately connected to the movement of the stock market.

I have been redeemed.

But this redemption was preceded by a terrible week. Everything I bought went down.; Then I bought more, and that went even further down. The prices of stocks were getting so ridiculously low, that I then bought more. Still, they went down. Soon I was totally margined and had no more money to buy. Still the stocks went down. I thought I would get a margin call. Finally, on Thursday, depressed and discouraged, I decided to give up on the whole stock market venture. I had taken out seven books on trading from the library. I brought them all back in disgust. I decided I would have to make money the "traditional" way, that is, by promoting my business. At least, I thought, it is something I am good in. The stock market stinks. I was wrong. I'll never succeed in making money at it. Give it up. Go back to work.

Fear, bordering on panic, visited me on Wednesday and Thursday. I saw myself once again losing all my money, ending up, if I was lucky, penniless, broke, sleeping on the sidewalk as a Bowery bum.

Then, suddenly, just as I had totally given up, the stock market turned around! And I, stunned, turned around with it.

What am I to make of this? I don't know. But I do feel glorious! And it is all because of an external event, the stock market upward move.

It this true? I needed confirmation of my direction. I've always loved the market. I don't like getting kicked in the teeth by my love. But that's exactly what it did. My angry lover kicked me in the teeth. And then, for some reason, she turned in my favor.

Is she an outside force? Or is she in me? Obviously, she is in me. The market is me. I am the market.

It connects me to my deepest feelings of fear, greed, and this morning, contentment. Today I am confirmed. Today I am right. It may only be for today, but it sure feels good. I'm going to ride this good feeling. However, even as I ride it, I know it won't last.

We'll see how long I remember this.

I compare my fight to make money in the stock market with Garibaldi's struggles to unite Italy. The vicissitudes, the ups and downs of the stock market struggle with the vicissitudes, the ups and downs of Garibaldi's life.

Yesterday was an historic day. I sold all my Prudential account stocks. In saying goodbye to my long time broker, I closed both my personal and Keogh retirement accounts.

I closed them at a terrible loss.

The stock market has crashed. I foresaw a depression ahead. Then years of down market.

This is the first time in twenty-five years that I am ut free of my stock broker as well. (I'm keeping the few stocks my fidelity account. We'll see about that.)

I am stunned, in shock, sad, mad, depressed. But right after I sold everything, I felt a whiff of elation. It was the "at last, I am free!" feeling.

In retrospect, my twenty-five years in the stock market was financially the worst decision I ever made. I have now a good opportunity to rip into myself, say what a fuck-up and miserable person I am. Losing so much money and piling up so much debt is a perfect opportunity to lambast myself. I feel sad, mad, miserable, stunned, shocked, and confused. It's the "Huh, what happened?" feeling. A devastating wake-up call. My World Trade Center just collapsed. My Iron Curtain, my Western Wall of Hope just melted down, crumbled, and been destroyed forever.

I stand among the financial ruins all alone.

Of course, I have always been alone. Only, in my imagination I had the hidden "unrealistic" hope that somehow, someday, and in some way the stock market would mysteriously rise and take care of me by making me rich. I admit it. I had naive dreams of riches through the stock market. That's why I hung on. Wealth, wealth, wealth. Protection, protection, protection. Security, security, security. . . and love all wrapped up in delicious bundles of money.

Well, it was a dream with many nightmares along the way. But it ended for good yesterday.

I am now starting over financially. I could also call this the beginning of a new adventure. Both of these are positives views, up-beat approaches. But, since I am basically an optimist, I'm sure I'll eventually see this financial debacle as an ending and a new beginning. Right now I'm focusing on the ending. I'm not ready to look ahead. That comes later.

A twenty-five year financial chapter has ended.

Making Money

Home at last.

I face bills and debts. How to pay it off—with no stock market hopes, no market miracles.

Probably my best bet for making money is through my own efforts. This means by working. I am my own best ticket to higher funds.

It is a slow, unsure, unsteady route. But it is the only route!

I just returned from Spain. Hard to believe how good I'm feel about selling all my stocks!

Performance

Return to Music

What are the signs that it is time to return to music?
1. Guitar: Finger nails growing back.
2. Scottish bagpipe: Influenced by gaita.
3. Accordion: Influenced by Paul.

All the above took place in Spain. Classical guitar was born in Spain. My ideas came in Santiago de Compostela, home of Segovia's summer master classes. I also solidified the Scottish bagpipe idea through my decision not to purchase a Galician gaita in the Santiago de Compostela music store. I solidified the accordion playing idea as well.

The Pilgrimage across northern Spain ends in Santiago de Compostela. Could one of the results of the walking its Camino be a return to music on a new and expansive level?

The New Guitar Concerts

Give concerts from my Teaneck living room. Radiate beauty, and repair the world with guitar vibrations.

I give visible and invisible concerts for the public.

In the visible world, I communicate to my concert audience through their senses. But during "in-room" concerts, when audience is invisible, I communicate ethereally, and send virtual musical messages directly into their souls.

The big difference between visible and invisible concert is: Invisible one are harder to hear.

Playing The Body

Playing the body with its meridians, chakras, and energy centers is similar to playing guitar.

First learn where to place your fingers. Then learn chords, strums, harmony, and theory. Soon you make music, and give a concert.

Giving a healing massage is like giving a concert on somebody else's body.

Stage Fright

Last night I decided to conquer stage fright.

Ha!

I say "Ha!" because it seems so preposterous, absurd, and impossible. Sure it's easy to study psychology, practice mental exercises, read about incredible cures in books, and hear them from so-called experts. But in actuality, no matter how hard I practice, stage fright just doesn't go away.

I know this fear is a residue of the past. Big deal. Knowing this important bit of personal and factual knowledge has done absolutely nothing to help me conquer stage fright. Neither have hours of practicing guitar. I never practice singing. I go for months without practice; then I get on stage and sing without a problem. I practice classic guitar for hours, days, weeks, months, years; stage fright is still with me.

What can I do about it?

Dive into it! This sinking, terrifying feeling that I will forget my pieces and sink into an oblivion of public humiliation, never leaves me. The only way of handling it is: enter the lion's mouth every time I play in public. My fighting tools are technical skills and the courage to enter, hover over, and perhaps fall into the wide-jawed abyss.

After my concert Saturday night, I asked some members of the audience about stage fright. What did they think? What causes it? Can one escape its grasp? What, if anything, can one do about it? I got many answers. But the thing I noticed most is that no matter how many answers I got, I had been through them all before. No one had an answer for me. Then I realized that somewhere, deep down in my person, I knew how to handle stage fright. I was the only one who knew! But this knowledge had not yet risen to the surface.

It still hasn't. I don't know how to conquer stage fright. But at least I do know where to look: straight into my heart, straight into my soul, straight into the demons and residue of my psyche. I won't waste my time asking others. Unless, I just want to make conversation or have a psychological–philosophical discussion. After all, it is an interesting topic. But as for a visceral understanding, one that reveals the workings of my mind and may be actually useful, I will look straight into myself. No matter what horrors I find, at least I know I'm on the right path.

Does this mean I must put myself before audiences, test and practice courage in the only arena it counts, namely, the public arena?

This is a good reason to give concerts: to grow, expand, and fight the inner tiger.

Enter the tiger's mouth. Then ride the tiger! That's how I'll start.

Concert as Public Prayer

Guitar notes are grandeurs in themselves.
Even lowly legatos and rote scales.
Prepare a Concert.
See if I can "fall into God's arms"
And express awe-and-wonder,
Let my notes communicate stellar vibrations.
Let my concert be a public prayer.

Memory Slips are New Directions in Disguise

If I forget my Bach *Fugue* while playing a concert, do I need a quick exit, an escape plan? If I have one, I can save myself from embarrassment?

Do I need an escape from slips of memory?

It is better to see them as new directions in disguise.

Self-expansion is the hidden purpose behind memory slips.

Beyond Segovia

Beyond Segovia!

I am going beyond mentors and heros, leaving them behind as I walk the lonely, righteous, uncertain, illuminated path straight into myself.

As I play guitar with serendipitous mistakes and sloppiness, new horizons open.

I am walking on the musical path of freedom.

Higher forces support me as I enter the Domain of Uncertainly

Concert Freedom

I gave a concert last night at the Paramount Hotel New Year's Weekend. I began with Villa-Lobos *Prelude Number 1*. I played it beautifully. I usually do. It is an excellent opening piece and easy for me to play. Then I moved on to Gaspar Sanz' *Pavane* and *Canarios*. I started to fall apart on that one. To recover, I began Malats' *Serenade* but continued falling apart. As I played, I fought my lack of concentration. But then something new and different happened. As my right hand froze and my body refused to relax, my mind said: "I'm tired of public anxiety bouts; I'm sick of fighting them." Then, right in the middle of the Malats' *Serenade*, I stopped playing, looked up from the guitar, and said, "But then Malats thought his *Serenade* wasn't romantic enough, so he decided to sing." I switched gears and sang the calypso "Love, Love, Love."

Although I was embarrassed from having failed in public, I hid it well. The audience probably thought I had "planned" this sudden change. Inwardly, I "knew" I had failed. Yet, somehow it didn't bother me. I vaguely realized that, rather than fail, I had suddenly and subtly opened up a new door. Imagine, embracing such a serendipitous change and all in the name of staying relaxed in public. I liked it. I was no longer chained to the concert order I had created. I was free to give the "concert of the moment," free to follow not only the spontaneous dictates of my inner voice, but also the higher orders of HaShem Himself. No doubt, He is the one who made me fall apart before others. He had a higher calling for me—be myself no matter how embarrassing or difficult it got. He even wanted me to get beyond nervousness, to worship Him fully by living totally in His present moment. Well, changing my concert order on the spot was the first step.

I improvised in the moment. I swam, twisted, turned, made up a few off-beat outlandish stories to "explain" my situation, and moved on. People loved it. I'm a professional and can handle public ups and downs easily on the surface, even thought inwardly they kill me.

But this time they didn't kill me; and I was smart enough to realize a new door was opening—the door of concert freedom.

Do something wrong for a change.
What exhilaration, fun, and joy!
Get used to it.

Notes Are People In Disguise

Notes are people in disguise.
Each note has an inherent integrity and speed.
Create, play, and express them.
Phrases, groups of notes, are like family.
In larger numbers, they become a concert audience.
Notes are the connecting bridges between private and public, performer and audience.

Play Softer

Play softer
On a whisper level
The gentle level
Quietly
Whisper into the deep open,
To levels beyond comprehension.
Ego washs away
A I take steps into the realm
Of Heart-Worship.

Questions are answers in disguise.

Master Dancer Teacher

A good dance teacher dances in his shoes.
A master dance teacher dances in the shoes of others.
His feet are in the Universal Shoe.

Reflections On A Weekend Concert

I read "A Real Fan" and "Depressions Can Be Fun." Reading them was a welcome addition to my concert program. So was singing "The Art Of Gargling" as an opener. Although I did feel some pressure to play classical guitar, it softened when I began my three Milan *pavanes* by introducing Luis Milan as one of the 16th century's outstanding garglers.

Once again during last nights program, ad-libbing stories and insane dialogue with my audience rolled so easily from my lips. It is my talent and joy. The lovely insanities leaking from my mind point to a wonderfully zany individual deep with. The pictures that pop into it truly delight me. Such as Hernando Cortez searching for a deli inside the Mount Popocatepetl volcano or visits with Joseph Stalin who loved singing Russian songs inside volcanos while holding shoulders—deltoids, of course—with Cortez, DeSoto, and other Spanish explorers.

These off-beat images rise wonderfully from the coiled depths of my twisted soul. They are beautiful absurdities that make life not only bearable, but lovely as well. They are my warm bubble bath on a cold rocky day.

Another way of playing classical guitar might be to start before the concert. Sit on stage while people walk in and just play. They can either listen or not. Then, when everyone is seated and "ready," I might just lift up my head, say hello, and start singing or even do a reading.

Submission

I am weary of self; the ego burden is heavy, indeed. How peaceful and lovely to hand my self over to a higher power.

I am best when I submit. Submit to the higher power when I play guitar, write, dance, lead a tour, or whatever.

The road of submission can be a beautiful path. Just thinking about it brings relief.

Submit to the voice of your talent, to the best in you, submit to that Great Self within.

Before a Concert

If an Indian sadhu (mystic, holy man) can concentrate his mental powers in his arm and hold it up for twelve years, I can focus on my inner strength for twelve minutes before a concert.

Nervousness And Vitality

There is hidden vitality in nervousness. Rather than forgetting, suppressing, or relaxing my way out of it, focus on its vitality.

The Beginning Of My New Life

Yesterday in Prague I heard a classical guitar concert given by Milada Karezova. Excellent performance.

The day before I went to hear a performance of the *Four Seasons* by Vivaldi. Excellent musicians.

Most surprising about both concerts was my reaction to them. Basically, I had no reaction. As I listened to the superb violinist play Vivaldi, my mind drifted into space. Soon I fell asleep. When the performance was over, I walked out relaxed.

I was puzzled. Why did these concerts have no affect? Usually during such performances I cry or mentally soar into the heavens. This time nothing happened.

Same with the classical guitar concert. Milada Karazova played beautifully. Excellent technique, a relaxed and beautiful right hand. She played Leyenda flawlessly with a wonderful arpeggio flow. In the past, I would walk out of such a concert sick with jealousy, wishing I could have such superlative technical abilities and be so comfortable in my playing ability. Attending a classical guitar concert usually made me sick with jealousy as I was forced to face, once again, all my guitar playing inadequacies.

But this time I felt no jealousy, inadequacy, no wish to be someone else, no flights of fantasy or imagination. I even fell asleep when she played the Villa-Lobos *Prelude Number One*.

What do these new feelings mean? Or rather, what do these lack of old feelings mean?

It is easier to give to others than receive their gifts.

It is difficult to receive and accept praise. I have to improve myself first. I must push to get better so at some future date I'll be worthy of receiving the "better person" award.

Receive a reward from others? Ridiculous. I act and smile graciously when accepting awards in public, but inwardly, a small voice whispers "You are not yet worthy."

That voice is fading.

Perhaps my lack of reaction to the concerts reflects this new state. Instead of punishing myself by thinking what an inadequate guitarist I am, how much I must improve, and how unworthy I am, I now begin to say yes!

It's a big jump from the "No!" and "Never!" of last year.

New pathways have been carved on this tour. Ready to return to America. Looking forward to starting beginning my new life.

Daring

As I play guitar, daring means missing the notes—even forgetting them. It is part of masculine Bourree playing.

Daring also encompasses looking backwards, exploring graveyards, reading tombstones headlines, sifting through in former deeds, and luxuriating in awe-and-wonder energy bursts.

The Awe-dience

Performing before an audience creates a sense of awe. What will their reaction be?

Facing the abyss: Before I perform, my dread twists between excitement and panic. A sense of awe enters my being carrying questions like: How did I get into this mess? What am I doing here? Where will this lead? When will this performance end? Will I get out of it alive?

What a frightening and magnificent creation is our universe!

It is good to perform and put myself in this vulnerable position. And this even though it scares the shit out of me. Isn't that part of awe? How awesome to stand at the edge of the cliff and peer into the abyss of infinity.

Awe, with its concomitant, wonder, is the nature of performing relationship, and even to the universe itself.

Nevertheless, I can't go around all day in a state of awe and wonder all day. Too exhausting. I need rest periods, long ones. Awe states are high points, the stars and sun, burning the brain as they point the way to the fiery land of Imagination.

What does this mean in terms of personal direction?

It means more public performances, concerts, and public reading. More placements before the awe-dience.

I no longer need to perform to prove or improve myself. Rather, I need it to frighten myself, empty my bowels and bladder, and fill the ensuing vacuum with wonder.

Awe and wonder indeed. In this sense, an awe-dience can be One-derful.

My route home is through song.

Patricio played violin, Marvin played mandolin, I played guitar and gaida, George sang "Cucurucucu." We all improvised and coordinated. Born from nothing, created from nothing, filled with serendipites, our program, rose and grew into a great evening concert of musical discovery and enchantment.

My route home is through song. Singing gives me the opportunity to improvise before an audience.

In the middle of the program, Phil asked that I play "something serious." I played *Serenade* my Malats. . .beautifully, slowly, and well. Everybody loved it. It was just enough classical guitar playing for a folk song evening (although I can see a future where I could play more classical pieces.)

I could have told Phil our songs were serious: seriously funny. In fact, all songs are serious, even the funny ones.

Songs are my public form of journal writing. Standing before my audience, I talk to them in public just like I talk to myself in private when I write my journal. Through mouth, tongue, throat, fingers, stomach, hands, liver, kidney, fingers, heart, soul, and other unseen inner organs. I create a universe on the spot.

I Need An Audience

The Grow Weekend taught me that I need an audience.
Simple as that.
I need one for my songs, guitar, writing, improvisation, weekends, tours, and folk dance classes. Without one, I am incomplete.
This proves that I must publish, give concerts, run weekends, teach folk dance classes, and reach out for customers.

Empty Carnegie Hall

I love the freedom of playing to an empty Carnegie Hall. Ah those beautiful empty seats. I sink my guitar playing teeth into their cushy bottoms! They are mine all mine, and no one can stop me!
What a sensual delight: an empty Carnegie Hall!

"Hod" and Glory

Hod means glory in Hebrew.
I play the "Alhambra." Carnegie Hall seats are slowly filling up with a new audience.
I don't understand this audience yet. But as I play the glorious, roaring, magnificent, elevating second part A major passage of the "Alhambra," soaring on the fingerboard up to new tremolo D heights, my new audience turns into hod. Glory!
My "Alhambra"–Jewish–Spanish–classical guitar connection.

Life At the Edge

Part of me wants to make mistakes during a concert. Taking chances puts me at the edge of the cliff. That's where excitement dwells.
Mistakes are part of the fun. . . if I can stand them.
Freedom from the tyranny and fear of making mistakes, liberates passion. Ecstasy in ebullient mode. Euphoria stabbing the earth in sunburst of molten white light.

My head spins as I play *Bulerias*. I'm still in charge but almost out of control. The ceiling falls. Fingers fly through the roof. I rocket upward, heading for the stars. Accented Bulerias beats and lighting piccados go wild. *Aaiee*, What a ride!

Stage Fright

Audiences frighten me.

The root of the word "awe" comes from the Hebrew "ire" which means "fear." Awesome, awful (awe-filled) means filled with the fear of God. His awesome majesty, awful might.

Now there's motivation! Stage fright might be just the spice I need to put more flavor into my life.

Improve

Can I get even better?

Yes!

Yes to the attempt, effort, and struggle.

What does "get better" mean?

Improve.

Treading the path of self-improvement will not only make me better, but will make me feel better, healthier, heartier, more wholesome, and bring sparks of light to my eyes.

Pain and fear are brothers working together on a personal motivational plan for mankind. They're busy creating the Universal Stimulant. It may not be pleasant to take their medicine but it can sure motivate you!

Frozen with terror, paralyzed by pain. These are the motivation killers. But when fighting forces of anger, indignant rage, self-worth, and personal dignity are mobilized, their power releases the Universal Stimulant. Soon its magic begins to work.

I need the pressure of an audience to release my stimulant.

Today there is nothing more glorious than playing "Recuerdos de la Alhambra!" Over and over again I play. It puts me in heaven.

Nothing could be better! Other details of this world are simply annoying.

I am there. I am here. I'm in "Alhambra" joy and ecstasy land. Where else is the to go? Nowhere. This is it!

How can I sustain and remember it?

Exhilaration Practice

I thought I aimed to play fast on the guitar. I was wrong. Secretly, unbeknownst to me, I was aiming to play with exhilaration.

The real meaning of "fast" is exhilaration.

Are the pains in my feet are subtle ways of resisting exhilaration through my feet, resisting the exhilaration of folk dancing and running? Could be.

Living in the Land of Bass

After years of living in the flitty land of Treble I am moving into the powerful, sustaining Land of Bass with its long-willed foundation tones, stable support, and certainty of purpose.

Sails Man

I am a sails man.

Guitar fingers sailing.

Flapping and rotating arms lift me high into eagle soaring realm. Spirits rise and fly. Yet pained feet pin me down, anchoring my body to the earth.

It is the nature of heightened consciousness to be opposed by contrary force, a negative pull in the opposite direction.

Soring

Do you have to get sore in order to soar?
Yes.

But once you soar, you no longer feel sore.
Soring is the channel for soaring.

New Singing Voice

I hesitate to release my singing voice in public. I'm embarrassed, shy, afraid someone will see my "real feeling." I'll expose the depth of my emotion, the crying beauty in my personal canto jondo. I'll make a fool of myself. Others will laugh at me.

I do not have to practice this voice. I have only to free it.

Dare I release it?
If I dare, I am there.

No wonder I hesitate to sing in public. I break down and cry so often for the sheer beauty of it. The songs are so emotional, so close and dear to my heart. They are the essence of my protected in-room beauty experience. The power of early Israeli songs! "Mi Barechev," "Yamin U Smol." I dare not present such raw beauty, such pristine, fragile, and frightening ecstasy in public. Hardly ever in private, either.

But now I'll dare.

How To Give A Concert

When teaching folk dancing I noticed that if I hold back, that is, eliminate fast Romanian-type dances, not only does my body ache and I get tired, but I lose my inspiration as well. Do not hold back. Give it all you've got. If this means I lose part of my audience, so be it. Doing fast Romanian-type dances in spite of people's "too fast!" complaints lifts the dance and aerobic level of the class. Fast, lively dancing is good for me. It raises my spirits. I cannot and should not teach a class without raised spirits.

Last night I added several fast-type Romanian dances to the folk dance class. It healed me and raised my spirits. I succeeded in spite of the fact that several people sat down.

Perhaps that is the way I should give concerts, too. Forget the audience. Remember, I am giving the concert first to please myself, second to please the audience. Naturally, the two go together. But in terms of priorities, pleasing myself comes first. You can't love another until you love yourself; you can't raise up the spirits of another until you raise your own.

Use the fast Romanian-type dancing concert approach.

It is a good way to handle nervousness and performance anxiety, too.

Pour on the juices! Give it all you've got! Fuck myself, and, in the process, fuck the audience, too.

Irene, Goodnight

Start my concert by singing "Irene, Goodnight." Ask for audience participation. Only three chords, simple to sing. Courage is demonstrated, but hardly any skill.

Would it be humiliating to start out so simply? What about proving myself, introducing myself with a bang, impressing them, showing my talents, wowing the audience with a virtuoso display of pyrotechnics? Shouldn't I prove I'm worthy of love and admiration by starting off with a classical guitar piece? Then, once done, I can relax and have fun.

This has been my former approach to performing, full of self-proving egotism.

The "Irene, Goodnight" approach is valid.

Classical Guitar For Private Pleasure

If I am going to be starting my performances with "Irene Goodnight," then classical guitar will played only for my personal pleasure! I don't need it for public performances anymore. (Actually, I never did.) Sure, I'll play one or two pieces in public, maybe the Milan *Pavanes*, *Romance D'Amor*, and perhaps a flamencan dance and Granados *Spanish Dance Number 5*. But I don't need to practice anymore to play them. Frankly, it doesn't matter if I ever play them in public. I don't need any classical guitar to make my appearances. It can now be played privately, for my own pleasure, meditation, and personal development.

Classical guitar can enter the category of yoga, running, language study, and all the other "useless," non-money making activities.

Reaping the Harvest

Reading Bob Dylan's book about the '60s is my way of reading about my own life in Greenwich Village during that time. I am amazed that I can look back and revisit the past somewhat calmly. Evidently, I now have more perspective.

Perhaps that is why things seem easy, flowing, and pleasant. All the years of hard work "have been done." I'm putting it all together now—reaping the rewards of all my labors, of a life time of work to perfect my arts.

Guitar is together, *New Leaf* is together, performance feels easy and flowing, the pressure of tour success is off, so is money pressure. All these streams of my life are flowing together. Slowly, into one long Mississippi River of Better, one long muddy and endless flow of River Bettermore.

I am at the doorway of a new place.

Is this what my birthday is about?

Gaida Enthusiasm

I played the gaida so well I decided to commit myself to daily practice. I sounded so good! I see hope and progress ahead.

Why not return to Bulgaria this summer? For lessons and inspiration? I'll take lessons with George, have a new bag made for my Maria gaida, hear more playing, and generally rekindle my interest and enthusiasm.

So, when Maya at Balkan Travel insisted that, in spite of my small group, I go to Bulgaria, I agreed. I'll call Sylvia. If she registers today, I'll run the trip.

Filled with a mighty purpose, I drove to her house, and, despite my reservations about her spaciness, mental wanderings, and possible advent of Alzheimer's or some other unknown disease, and that traveling with her might be a nightmare, I happily picked up her check.

My Inner Audience of Eternal Mothers

I am an outlaw.

I stand on the high peaks of the Alpujarra in southern Spain, shouting out my joyous freedom. The Granada audience below hardly hears me. But it doesn't matter. My inner audience, my internal cheering section, just love me!

They are the ones I play for.

What does an outlaw to do? He plays beyond the law. No one hears him plucking guitar in the wide-open spaces of the freedom-loving Spanish plains or the high wild peaks of the mountains. All alone in his glory, yelping with freedom and joy, there is no external public to applaud, no outer audience to see or experience his glory.

Even his mother is not there.

His inner audience, a standing room only crowd of internal mothers, cheer him wildly. "You are the outlaw of my dreams!" they cry. "We love you, every last virtual one of us! You dream us into existence and we, in turn, dream of only you! Play on, oh, wild one. We love your freedom! We love the abuses of your free-wheeling meanness. Put us down, put us up, put us perpendicular, or flat, vertical or sideways. It doesn't matter. We swoon for the smashing masculinity of your lawless freedom! Give it to us! We love it!"

Now these are women I can relate to! My eternal, internal audience of inner mothers with their unbounded love and admiration for my wildness, expansion, growth, and freedom!

Simply Silly

I am always playing for an audience. If this audience is an internal one, why bother spending so much time and effort courting the outer one, the so-called "public?"

Is there actually a public? Or is the public a fiction, a projection of my inner audience of mothers?

I live forever with this eternal, internal audience. I can never get away from them. Nor would I want to.

As for my outer audience, my so-called "public," well, they come and go. They are like ghosts wafted by the wind, fictions blowing past me, sitting down on my stoop for a short drink, then moving on to who knows where.

Why pay attention to the vicissitudes of this virtual audience when my real audience lies within? Of course, it's polite to acknowledge them with a brief hello. But more attention than that is not only time consuming but annoying as well. It is simply silly.

Performing As "Writing In Public"

Moses talks to God. God talks to Moses. Moses tries to please God by doing what He says.

Although He is often pushy, God accepts Moses' actions even when he does not accomplish all of His commands.

God is a nice guy.

Moses tries hard.

Where does this discussion taking place? In Moses' heart. That is where God lives. Moses talks to the One within.

A secularist might say Moses is rationalizing his explanations, putting God's stamp on his own thoughts to give them an extra punch.

What does all this have to do with me?

Well, once my idols crumbled, I was left with only God to rely on. Where is He? Within. Thus when I speak to Him and discuss issues, I am actually talking to myself. Schizophrenic, you say? Well, maybe. But God has many characters, and so do I.

Last night I heard Sigrid Erickson perform at the Redeemer Church in Dumont, New Jersey. She sang second half of the concert. The first half was given by a flutist.

While the flutist performed, I thought: I should be up there performing. By not giving concerts, I am chickening out, denying myself a big challenge. Performing is so terrifying for me, so hard. I can't stand the nervousness I feel before going on stage. Only money seems to distract me from this fear. If I am not paid, I won't go through the torture of performing.

What is the prime reason for such performing anxiety? High expectations for playing the classical guitar. If I gave that up, only sang, talked, led group singing, clowned, joked, ad libbed, stood up only to smile, then performing might be "easy." Yes, that's the word I used: easy! I might actually enjoy it! Performing would become "writing in public."

Yes, writing in public! This means giving a spontaneous performance. Just like the spontaneous performance I give when I sit down at my computer to ad lib and improvise with language. My writing is an exercise in improvisation, spontaneity, and instant creation. I love it. I am talking about the key to not only future performances, but, more important, how I can actually enjoy the adventure of performing!

Connecting Link

Truth is, the only thing that gets me to sing and play guitar is an upcoming public performance. This means performing is always in back of my mind. It is part of my practicing... and practice.

Performing is a hidden element in my daily practice.

If part of me secretly wants an audience, then it has always been a secret part of my miracle schedule. It is my desire to be heard is thus the ultimate, kabbalistic connection between ego and audience, inner self and outer self, I and thou.

I hesitate to face this hidden aspect of myself. Too traumatic.

What was the trauma? Non-responsiveness to my outlandish offbeat humor, love of the absurd, and even to the beauty expressed through classic guitar playing. My off-the-wall fliers like Jewish Skver Densink vit some Kuntri ent Vestern led by Jacov Gelt might be subject to audience blank stare of non-responsiveness.

If I go public and the non-responsive trauma hits me, can I take it?

I have no choice. Hiding is no longer an option.

Public as Energizer

Instead of fighting them off, closing the door of my inner room, walling myself off in my private, artistic chamber to protect myself from their invasion, see the public as an energizer.

An audience energizes me!

Slow and soulful is a pathway to practice.

"Dropping" Classical Guitar

After the great success of the LOV (Land of the Vikings) Weekend Saturday night sing along, I can see how unnecessary it is for me to play the classical guitar.

If that is the case, why should I practice now? To what purpose? I'll have to find a new reason. The old one is dead.

Or, is it time to drop it completely? Gulp.

Does it fit in anywhere? Isn't it now merely a sideline in an evening of music, of folk songs, ad libs, readings, group songs, etc? I could get by, easily get along without it. Sure, it's a nice thing to throw a classical piece or two into a program. But if I don't, that's fine too.

The performance of classical guitar has lost its significance and importance to me. Indeed, I hate to say it, but after so many years of practice, of hours spent on the "Alhambra" and more, I am ready to drop it!

What a downer. But also an entry into new freedom.

Should I practice anymore?

I don't know.

Destruction As Part of Creation

I practice the Villa-Lobos *Number Four* arpeggio over and over again. It the beginning it is slow and smooth, in the middle, still smooth. But by the end, it is fast and choppy. I have moved from smooth flowing creation to fast choppy destruction.

Is the goal of practice to reach destruction? Creation? Both? Do I want to destroy what I create, in order to create what I destroy?

No doubt part of this morning's Villa-Lobos practice was to destroy what I created. Thus why be afraid of choppiness and mistakes? Why fear destruction in general? In a perverse way, that is what I am striving for.

Indeed, creation and destruction are the Creative process.

Relaxation Hints

The relaxation in my body tell me how to play the arpeggios in Villa-Lobos' *Prelude Number 4*.

Listen to the body during other arpeggios, in calliyoga, and in general.

Listen to relaxation hints within. They point the way.

The Dark Power Hidden Behind The Index Finger

Reaching with the index finger feels so good.

What is the attraction to reaching with the index finger? It is reaching all the way back into my potential.

It is reaching into a dark, sexual energy type of power. Very mysterious and somewhat frightening. Tinged with awe. I am attracted to its mystery but also frightened by it.

Business

Numbers Make Excitement!

Great Bedford class! What have I learned?
1. Numbers make excitement!
2. Build my classes through registration. Use the Bedford and Darien method for Monday and Tuesday night. Register students for series. $10/class for members. Others pay $15 (or $12) at door.

Mailing Lists

Should I have a mailing list, give it up, or simply do a mailing once a year?

How about doing only selected mailings to people who have attended weekend, tour, or dance class?

These special mailings, on specialized lists, would also go to agents, people who have booked me, bar mitzvah people, etc. I would limit each list to under one hundred people.

I could have two lists. A general list for every customer. I'd mail to them once a year.

The second list would be specialized. I'd mail to this list several times a year, for special events.

This means often entering some people's addresses two times. But I'd only do it for the ones who have attended a weekend, a tour, or booked me.

In summary: I'm thinking about specialized lists and specialized mailings again. I'm personalizing everything for the important customers, those who support my business.

Business means taking my vision public.

Everything is going well. Not only going well, it's going very well. Why did I wake up sad this morning?

It began a week ago when I heard flamencan guitar played on the radio. I cried remembering the beauty of last year's tour to Andalusia. Wonderful experiences, wonderful job, wonderful organization. Wonderful tour. How sad that, due to lack of registration, I'm not running tours.

Then as I sat in my car listening to the music of the Spanish soul, tears streaming down my face, a sudden decision came to mind: Despite possible money loss and low-to-no registration I would run my tour to northern Spain anyway! These tours are just too exciting not to go on. They are good for my physical and mental health, and they are certainly good for my soul. They must never be abandoned simply because business stinks, there are no registrants, and the tour market does not support them. Winds of business blow hot and cold, vicissitudes of life blow the same. Personal valor and commitment are beyond fickle movements of fate. Can faith conquer fate? Maybe, maybe not. But it can come close. Since we never know what our fate is anyway, at least we can maintain confidence, personal attitude, and belief in our faith. (Also there is still the possibility our faith can effect fate. Does it? Who knows? But at least, through faith and confidence in inner self and vision, you will be in charge.) Attitude rules mind even as vicissitudes from the outside world crash down upon it.

Can faith and fate intertwine? Do they effect one another?

Well, here's what happened: Once I decided to take fate into my own hands and commit myself to the Spanish tour by saying "I'm going there no matter what!" miraculous things began to happen. When I got home I found a letter from Ann Dini of California in my mail box. It had two deposits for my Spanish tour! And this after she told me the tour cost too much money. I had then done a great sales job with her. I said my tours are not for everyone. Some dislike them, others love them. Some have gone on all of them. Since you don't know my tours, I'd like to offer you a first-time reduction of $100 to $200 per person. Then you can judge for yourself. Ann said her husband was the one who was balking. She said she'd discuss it with him. I decided I had done all I could, hung up the phone, and mentally crossed her off. Then, to my utter amazement and pleasure, she registered!

One hour later, the phone rang. It was June Morse from Florida. Both she and her husband decided they now wanted to go to Spain, too and would send me a deposit! Instant happiness! Suddenly, my tour was on!

An hour ago, I said I would go with just two people. Now I had five! Since the tour was now alive I could get on the phone and tell all my former tour participants! I was back in the fight, back in business!

Next day Edith and Kjell Ring emailed me. They want to go to Croatia and will send a deposit. That Monday night, Gene and Nina Katz gave me deposits for Croatia! I called Audrey Shields and Robie Ancona. They're considering Spain, too. My travel world was lighting up again!

I had committed myself to my Spanish tour. My vow had been based on love and faith. Did my attitude effect the outside world? Love, coupled with desperation, can send out powerful vibrations. Had my mental waves, subtly but forcefully effected the workings of God's universe? I'll never know for sure but it certainly would be nice to think so.

I am overwhelmed by all my folk dance jobs. I am now teaching almost every day of the week; if you add my bar mitzvahs and wedding bookings, I'm teaching weekends, too.

I can feel overwhelmed or excited. I'll choose excitement.

Mark Twain said: "I'm an old man. I've had many problems. Most of them never happened."

Deepening the Tour Vision

Tours: I may start repeating myself. After new destinations of Norway, Sweden, and Iceland, I'm considering returning to Sicily, Greece, Turkey, even Israel.

I've done all the countries I love. Where else is there to go? What else is there to do? Return to them. Deepen my knowledge of their language and history.

It's like playing the guitar. I spent many years putting together a concert program, learning the pieces I like, memorizing the music I want to play. Now I know them. I have no desire to learn new guitar pieces. What else is there to do but play this music I love over and over again. In the process, I deepen my knowledge, love, and wisdom.

Perhaps tourism it is the same thing. Like a concert, I now have a repertoire of tour countries.

Taking Credit

After a good night's sleep in Lugo, we arrived in Galicia.

Tough tour. Great people. I love it! I'm in an expansive mood.

Today I want to do more! More tours, more push-ups, more, more, more.

This tour has gone well on so many levels. Great people, great guide in Mayte, great me. I even survived yesterday's claustrophobic, pit-of-the-stomach panic.

Can I take credit for having great people, great Mayte guiding, great going public, and great tour?

Well, why not? I am the leader. I do create the mood. I've had so much fun being my expansive, off-the-wall, running wild self. My personal victory is that I've done all in front of others! The few times I've been criticized, I've checked my mind, realized its potential lid formation, conquered it through awareness, gone past it, and moved on. Many instances where I could have simply shut up and shut down. But I didn't shut up or shut down. Instead, I kept going! I broke through enclosed walls, smashed plastic lids. Good for me! Gone public! The coalescing result of psychoanalysis and birth of the New.

I'll take credit. This tour has been my creation. Sure I've had help from Mayte, her father, Paco, agent Alejandro, and my fine tour members; of course, I could not have done it without them. But the fact that I need them does not take my credit away. Just as a writer needs a pen as an instrument to create his writings, so I need Mayte, Paco, Alejandro, and my tour members to create this tour. They are instruments in my hands just as I am an instrument in God's hands. Through me, and my tour members, God makes Himself manifest in the world.

Tours are fun!

Big headache last night. That's two in a row. I'm missing something here.

Although I love this tour group, I am still the leader. That means that, even though I am having fun, my responsibilities while on tour, never end! This sets me apart from everyone else. Always. Thus my love for the group and the fun I'm having is qualitatively different from everyone else.

On tour, while leading a tour, I am always working. My responsibilities go on night and day and last the entire two weeks. I can never get away from them. Nor should I. No do I want to.

I like my responsibilities, They can be fun. But they are also a constant weights on my shoulders. Aha, weight on my shoulders, on my neck. . . and head! That is what is causing my headache. We approach the end of this tour. I am tired. I've had enough. I need an escape, a rest, a vacation. I'm ready to go home. But I've still got a few days to go. So I'm feeling a bit trapped. But, until now, I was not aware of this feeling. Result: a splitting headache.

What can I do about this?

1. Be aware. Recognize the claustrophobic panic of feeling trapped. That fear is physically "expressed" in my headache.

Panic? Did I say panic?

Claustrophobia? Did I say claustrophobia?

Trapped, stuck in the closet, dropped into a well, squeezed in a vise. These are some feelings I have at the end of a tour.

The only cure for panic, claustrophobia, stuck, and trapped is awareness. Awareness will cure me.

I'm not cured yet. But I've taken the first step.

Touring

One way to keep customers from complaining on tour is keep them so busy that they have no time to complain.

Practice it on the Croatian tour.

On folk dance class: You walk in feeling miserable and walk out feeling great.

My Business

I want to stuff myself with schedule so full I can't breath.
Why?
Working hard is really so good for me.

Thus push my business to the hilt! This includes writing and bookings (guitar, songs), exercises, and tours.

Passionate Love of Business

What do I love about business?

Formerly, I saw it as so worldly, foreign, concrete and people-oriented. People used to symbolize lids on my creativity. That concept has collapsed. By allowing myself the two-hour gifts of writing and exercise I have somehow lifted the business lid. I feel free. I opened the door to passionate love of business.

Passionate? Indeed, that is a radical new concept of business. It goes beyond love. It is passionate love.

Why would I have a passionate love of business? It has to do with a passionate love of people. I have a hidden passionate love of people. It is coming out in the open now. I no longer see a critical inner audience. My imagination has destroyed them, disintegrated these old symbols. In their place walks a new freedom.

Why does my body ache? Growing pains. I am destroying my old body and creating a new one in its place.

I wonder if business is the hidden, kabbalistic word for "people."

It's all about passionate love and letting it roll, free flow, and run wild across the lawn.

Joy in Problem Solving

Handling problems can become its own high.
How do you find joy in the process of problem solving?
Dive right into them.

I'm deflated over the Croatian tour fiasco.
What can I do? Fight for the terms of the original contract.
Actually, this situation is a threat to Paul, our relationship and future business dealings. Even though he was not present during the negotiations, Bill is still his employee. If I cannot trust what is in his

written contract, and terms can be changed at the last minute, then how can I do future business with him? This has to be straightened out.

The key word here is written. Written "contract" letter. Anyone can say "We spoke about it," or "I told you." But if it is not down on paper, how can it be proven. And of course, I based my prices on the written contract letter.

According to the original contract letter I would have made $4,026 profit. I counted this into the original price and expected to make it. By suddenly raising the final price I have been forced to pay an addition $4,026. This is totally unjust and wrong.

I must fight for my original contract and my $4,026. To be fair, I should at least get close to it.

What is my bargaining chip with Paul? Our business relationship. That is my bargaining chip. Our future business is on the line. Future business with him. It is in his self interest to straighten this out. (Mine too, of course.)

What have I learned for the future beyond this miserable incident?
1. I should handle all negotiations, schedules, monies, etc myself. Do not hand them over to Bill, Paul or anyone else. It is too time consuming and complicated. Plus I can make more money if I do it myself.
2. Be more specific in future contracts. Make sure as much as possible is written down and specified. Especially prices.

I can start applying these new skills of exactness in written contracts with next year's Norway and Sweden tour.

Screwed!
So this is what it feels like to get screwed.
Suddenly, Bill raised the price of our tour $400.00 per person. He neither warned nor consulted me. I looked at our contract. It says nothing about such a price. No matter how many times I read it, try to understand it, him, or how such a misunderstanding could take place, I can't find anything in this written document to support his new price. He says he told me about it. I don't remember being told.

Besides, even if he did, what we discussed should have all been in writing. It wasn't. That is the problem.

This screw up has been bothering me for days. I spoke to Paul about it. Although he is the boss, he said he wasn't present for my negotiations. That is true. Nevertheless, as boss, he is responsible. A contract should have been written clearly stating the prices, then okayed by me. Well, I do have a contract letter. It does state a price. It is the only written document that has passed between us. I based my tour price on it. Then suddenly, at the last minute, Bill raises it by $400 per person.

No matter how I twist and turn, trying to rationalize or understand Bill's new price, I cannot accept it. It is simply not right.

At best Bill was sloppy; at worse, amateurish. Actually, both. I don't believe he was trying to be dishonest or to put one over on me. I am too long term a customer. I've had good relations with Paul for almost twenty years. This is the first time I have ever worked directly with Bill. It is also our first tour to Croatia and Slovenia. Nevertheless, whether it is the first or last time, there should always be a written contract clearly stating the prices. There wasn't. That is the whole problem.

Mike must have realized something was wrong with this. Otherwise, why would he agree to give me $500? But his check really doesn't right the wrong of it. Nor do see any middle ground here. I am either right or wrong. They are either right or wrong. If I am right, I should get the complete $4,000 back. If I am wrong, I should return the $500 payment. Period.

Best for now is consulting a lawyer? Am I right? Am I wrong? Is there a middle ground? What, if anything, should be done? What are my options? These are the next questions. Jim is a lawyer. I'm calling him tomorrow.

I Know It Is True!

Whack, whack, whack! Smack, smack, smack! One day seems worse than the next. I'm descending into the maelstrom. My confidence is getting shot down. I'm getting scared. Vicissitudes are killing me. One messy and miserable and knock down after another.

Yesterday morning it was swollen feet and the Bill thing. By late morning I had added the Berger tour annoyances which reminded me once again of the Bill fuck-ups. Finally, a group of us went to an Indian restaurant for lunch and I fractured my tooth on a chicken bone. The whole incisor broke off in my mouth leaving a gaping hole. I was lucky to find a dentist, Dr. Kay, that very afternoon. He said I'd need a crown and post. The crown would cost $900, the post $300. Then I payed him his $125 entrance fee. That Indian lunch cost over $1,300. Plus there's the added annoyance of spending time next week at the dentist's office getting this tooth fixed. First, I lose $4,000 at Bill's fuck up, then another $1,300 at the dentist. That's over $5,000 down in ten days. Who knows what other expenses are going to come up. Add them to my usual pre-tour anxieties and the result is a stunning fall of confidence and the "everything is suddenly going wrong" feeling. Intellectually, I know this is not true. Yet, who's intellectual?

It seems everywhere I turn now there is a sudden added, unforeseen expense. They're piling on my head, pushing me down, adding to my debt, and slowly destroying my confidence.

But a sudden idea just occurred. Suppose financial miseries, aches, and pains are better than anxiety about success. What a thought! I can't see any success in the $5,000 worth of expenses I've just incurred, the sudden mounting of my debt, or in cracking my tooth. Yet I know that success anxiety is my bottom line crusher. It pushes my spirit into the grave. I can handle vicissitudes as long as I maintain my spirit. But without spirit, not only do vicissitudes fall by the wayside, but I fall with them. Crushed spirit equals zero.

Whacking a mind and body is a terrible thing. But whacking the spirit is worst of all.

Financial blows are knocking me down. But, and here's a good thought: So what? What else is new here? I've always been able to handle my problems and move on. Why should today be any different?

Ease, Simplicity, and Relaxed Are In

My tour of Slovenia and Croatia is coming up. I have the usual pre-tour concerns. How shall I approach them?

With ease.

Here are some to practice on.

1. Air tickets and vouchers are supposed to be here Wednesday. They have not yet arrived. Will I and my customers receive their tickets in time?

2. Will I have time to do all pre-tour preparation?

Stay calm and focused while the sea around you is boiling.

I'm leaving for Slovenia and Croatia today.

If I practice thinking certain thoughts for years, even a lifetime, naturally I will get better at thinking them. They will become habits.

I am talking about changing habits, longtime habits, life time habits of thought and attitude.

Habits of thought:

1. Alhambra: Go from "I can't play it" to "I can."

2. ours: I can run them with focus and calm. This creates ease. Customers will appreciate their tour leader.

3. Elations and depressions: See emotions as vicissitudes, passing phenomenon. Watch, accept, and "breathing into" them.

The above are good thoughts to ponder during my Slovenia/Croatian tour.

Solve Problems. . . One at a Time

Patience, fortitude, and slow stick-to-it-iveness slowly bring solutions. Some problems can be solved immediately, some take hours or days, some take weeks, months, even years to solve.

Beauty and Unity (Making Money Is A Sideline)

What will help me rise above my worries? Realizing the beauty of the Slovenia/Croatia adventure, of the human relations I improved, and of welding people together in a unified group.

I was put in the world with a purpose: To create beauty and unity. That is my talent. Making money is a sideline.

I Love My Tours!

It's Saturday morning. I feel slightly down. Why? I've come to the end of my tour and tour-ending energy cycle. I love my tours. I love my tour business! I feel a love down!

How can I respond to it?

Keep loving!

Then create more tours! Perfect the ones I've got. Use my enthusiasm to find new customers.

I will refuse to let any problem or worry spoil my fun, destroy inspiration, or cloud my joy.

Truth is that dealing with all the problems on tour was just so much fun! Exhilarating, exciting, challenging!

What a great attitude. I'm so lucky to have developed it.

New Dimensions

What pleasure I gave my customers on this tour.

Last night in Dubrovnik I practically fell asleep at the Lado concert. I was simply too tired to enjoy it; in my opinion the dancers were "okay." Yet my people loved it—and me for bringing them there. Same with dinners. They thanked me for bringing them to each restaurant. "They're good," I agreed. "But it's a surprise to me, too. After all, Bill from our tour company arranged the restaurants." But they thanked me anyway. Well, if I take the blame if it is a bad restaurant, why not take the credit if it is a good one?

What did I do to create the restaurant and dinner experience? I created the tour! Thus, even thought I cannot know every detail will work out in advance, I am responsible for what happens.

People will either enjoy or not enjoy my creation. Since I love appreciation for my writing or concert, why not love appreciation for my tours, weekends, and folk dance classes.

Tours are business expressions of my creative life. That's how business connects to the miracle schedule.

Some rewards are a hearty "Thank you!", "I love it!" or "What a great experience!" More subtly and indirectly: "I'm having so much fun." or simply a laugh or a smile.

Mitzvah Magic!

Joe got sick. I called him in his room. "How are you?" I asked. "I'm so glad you called," he said.

I looked up the bus schedule to Orobic for his wife, Sue. I helped them. How happy and appreciative they were.

What good feelings I get from helping others. Best of all is the magnificent mitzvah melt-down. I fly after I do a good deed! Mitzvah magic is the ultimate kick.

Business is about helping others. Anyone can help others. But you rarely consider how much fun it is!

The fun aspect of helping others is often disparaged. Selflessness is considered best. "I'm doing it for you." But, truth is, I'm doing it for me—and you! (I couldn't do it without you, and you couldn't have it without me. A perfect duet.)

Mitzvah magic creates the ultimate us, giver and receiver, helper and helped. What can you do but glory in this equation!

Making the Right Decision

We had the Brad and Lucille fiasco. I say fiasco but it was actually an annoyance, a leadership annoyance.

Time was tight. We had a restaurant appointment at 8:00 p.m. Brad and Lucille wanted to go back to the hotel. But time would not allow it. Then I found out they merely wanted to change clothes and take a shower! It would take too long. Plus it would inconvenience the whole group. Everyone else had no problem with going straight to the restaurant. I made a decision: Go straight to the restaurant. I couldn't inconvenience the whole group for one person (Lucille) who merely wanted to change clothes and take a shower. She could change in a local bathroom if she wanted, just like June and Diana.

Brad and Lucille were furious. Brad commented: "It's not right. We're paying a lot of money for this tour. We should be able to have dinner comfortably." I agreed with him. But because of prior commitments and time constraints, I couldn't accommodate him. Actually, his impatience and comments were childish, peevish, and disgusting. But I passed over these personal feelings, saying to myself,

I can understand why they're pissed off. I am, too. But what can you do? I "had to do what I had to do." Brad agreed.

Nevertheless, my decision got them mad as hell.

I dislike when my customers are mad at me. But as leader, it was my call. I had to decide. As adults, they could have realized the group situation and been more gracious. But they were not.

Well, for me, the buck stops here. I felt bad even though I made the right decision.

But I also felt proud of myself. In spite of the pressure, I made the right decision!

Leaning towards increased self worth. On one side comes frustration and disappointment from being unable to please them; on the other, pride in handling the situation, making the right decision, doing the right thing, and best of all, pride of effort from trying to do the right thing.

All A's

I paid for Berger's supper to smooth the waters.

That's the power of money. I can always pay!

"You said you would ask for fish, " Jack said at our farewell dinner in Split.

I answered. "Not true. I did it once. The voucher said kosher. . .or vegetarian, not fish."

I said, you said. Said, said, said. Even Bill said. Everyone uses "said" to support themselves in arguments of right and wrong. Bill also said. . . and I lost thousands.

It must be written down. Contracts must be exact.

Nevertheless, there are grey areas on tour. Every detail and event cannot be written down or included in a contract. It must be handled on the spot using judgement.

True, I never thought of asking for fish, nor was I supposed to. It was not my responsibility. Still the pain of Berger's demands falls on my shoulders. It may not be my responsibility but somehow I am the one who has to handle it.

In retrospect, maybe I should have let him pay for it. But I wanted, needed, and deserved peace during our last night's supper.

I bought inner peace by paying for their meal. It was also a good will gesture. (Plus, I may be able to get some of the money back through Livak's four missed Split meals. Thus financially, I may end up okay.)

If I had it to do this meal over again, what would I do?

1. I would never have asked the restaurant for fish. It would never have entered my mind.

2. I handled their tantrum appropriately and in place.

3. Only the payment question remains. Even there, the idea of switching finances was a good one. However, they should have paid and given me the receipt. Instead they balked at the payment, so I ended up paying for them and handling it.

This has two parts to it:

It was a good financial switch idea. It may succeed on a no loss or minor-loss basis.

The fact that I ended up paying rather than they. Here I felt slightly bullied. But I wanted, nay needed, to smooth Berger's ruffled waters. Perhaps even this was a good idea!

1. I created good will.

2. I made the right choice. Brad might have resisted paying anyway, which he did. I sensed his resistance and more trouble ahead. Instinctively, I headed him off at the pass by paying for his meal. Good intuitive thinking.

I'm coming out all pluses. New neighborhood thinking is coming in strong. All A's!

Another question: Do I want to create good will with the Bergers? Do I ever want them on tour with me again? Or are they simple too difficult?

Yes, I'd like to try one more time. I like them in spite of the trouble they are giving me. Plus dealing with their problems is a tour and personal challenge. It's also good for my writing. Look at all the pages I just turned out!

Through writing I just figured the whole Berger thing out. Through mere money I created good feelings. (By buying wine, too.)

Through mere money I handled resistance.

For mere money I bought instant good will. What a good, wise use of money!

Good will lasts for days, months, even years. Mere money payments are forgotten almost instantly.

Serendipity (in tourism or anywhere else) is hard to find because in order to get it you have to give it up.

Love Of Business

When I was five years old I played at the fountain in the park outside our house; I squirted water and made rivers in the mud. Down them I sailed little paper mercantile boats.

Playing in the park: That's business!

I love business.

The excitement and beauty of creating an event: Business is not a dry accountants pursuit but a passionate love affair!

Business: The Love Connection

Checks are love in the mail.

Customers open themselves up to me. They trust and have enough faith in me to give me their money. Money is a symbol of their love.

The money my customers send me is their love energy.

Money also symbolizes power: the power of connection.

The power of connection is Love.

Enthusiasts!

Enthusiasts are my support system. They support my cause and my business.

Although they are not my family, they are my friends. The distinction between friends and enthusiasts is an artificial one. The separation between business from goodness is based on the "Christian-communist" hate-money, anti-materialistic, dualistic philosophy of the separation between good and evil. A Manichean dualism in modern garb.

When I call enthusiasts in the morning, I am really calling my friends.

Ours is a visceral, down-to-earth, mutual support system.

Creating The Freedom To Compartmentalize

Yesterday I was redeemed with five tour registrations! It was my best day in five weeks. All the people came from my telephone calls. Results! My calls worked! Calling is my best sales tool. But, of course, I also need all the other ammunition.

Calling as in "I Have A Calling"

Hard to believe, but calling has entered my miracle schedule. Notice I do not use the word "business" or "sales" but calling.

What is calling?

It is a path.

It can be a plea for help.

But there is also the call of leadership as in "Come on, I've got something great for you!"

The word "sales" focuses on product or service. "Calling" is personal. One on one. It goes straight to the heart.

I am a caller.

My calling is for enthusiasm. En-*theos*-ism. Filled with *theos*. Calling has God connection within it. A people connection, too.

Folk Dance Ad:

Millie "Tuckerprimp" Globert, millionaire shopping magnate, saleswoman, and past president of High Percent Stripe Shoes, writes in Circle To Heaven Folk Dance Magazine: "I'm in a high pressure sales job. I spend hours on the road. Every day I try going somewhere, getting somewhere, moving ahead, getting ahead, staying ahead. My fun quotient is only at 17 percent. That makes me eighty-three per cent miserable. However, since I started folk dancing, my happiness has increased from seventeen to ninety-six percent! Folk dancers never go anywhere. They dances in circles! It's so beautiful when we all dance in a circle and go nowhere together!"

Since the invention of folk dancing in 9692 B.C., 86 percent of all folk dancers have been going in circles. Why be left out?

Our folk dance group embraces diversity and all political parties. Left, right, forwards, or backwards, even diagonals. We do them all. We have special arrangement with universal forces. Every time we jump, we come down. You will too. And have great fun in the process!

Running Wild On My Business Lawn

As I drove up to the Fallsview Hotel(now Nevele Grande) ideas hit me left and right. First idea: Use my *New Leaf Journal* as a folk dance journal. Publish bits, parts, or all of it in whatever order; use it to promote folk dancing! Aha, now here's an idea: Not only do folk dancers dance, they do yoga, write, read books on mysticism, religion, and philosophy, play guitar, sing, travel and tour. They do many and most of the things I do. If they don't, at least they are interested in them. That is why they are my friend-enthusiast-customers. My journal is just right for them. Many are in therapy, suffer in their own special way, laugh, cry, scream, get depressed or elated. They are like me. Therefore, my thoughts would appeal to them; my *New Leaf Journal* could be viewed as a sales tool, a personal folk dance voyage into the folk dance mind.

Another idea: At the lunch table in the dining room my conversation with Peggy, Aaron, and Mrs. Radish ended up with this superlative idea: a folk dance teacher's course. Peggy immediately said she would sign up. That's one. But the problem is once people learn to teach, whom will they teach? They have to start their own group. Most people don't want to do that. Some just want to "expand their practice." But, even beyond that, since I introduced my Gala Folk Dance and Four-Week Mini Course now I could have follow-through: namely, people from my folk dance course could follow through and teach that four-week mini course. They could start groups in synagogues, churches, organizations, and basements everywhere. They would expand folk dancing and, in the process, be part of my organization and plug into my weekends and tours. This is a brilliant way to get new customers, friends, and enthusiasts, and make money in the process. This idea is so brilliant I can't stand it. I'm trying to forget it like crazy. We'll see how long I can. But it has such an inevitable logic to it. Of course a mini course will work; and of course I'll find some kind of teachers to follow through; and of course, they'll promote my weekends and tours in the process; and of course the folk dance market, the base of my business pyramid, will expand.

This is an "of course" situation. But remember, I assumed this kind of incredible success when my books were published and when I started my tour business. I thought, wow, how can these miss? My books are great; my tours are great; everyone will flock to them. I can't help but become a millionaire. Well, that didn't happen.

My enthusiasms have been knocked so often I have become a shade cautious. The distance between dream and reality is farther than I thought. It takes mucho work to get there.

Or does it? Should I simply ride on the wings of my enthusiasm and the hell with the rest? Why not? I'm too old to work, but I'm not too old to play. I don't mind playing at work. But I still can't stand working at play. Therefore, I'll run wild on my business lawn!

All Communication Is Self-Communication

What is communication?

True communication is self-communication. You discover and understand yourself through others. They are a bridge to the country of self.

On a deeper level, the deepest level, the "other" is not a bridge. The "other" is you! All is one.

Sales is another way of communicating with yourself. It fosters the notion that all-is-one. By expanding the definition of self to include others, it brings them into your circle, widens it, and expands your conception of self.

Paradoxically, when I make sales calls, I am really calling myself.

There is no separation between my sales self, my "real" self, and my customers. All three are one. Tripartite. All is One.

Customers As Hidden Aspects Of Yourself

In sales, you try to find the right customer and give them what they want.

But, on a deeper level, you try to find the right hidden aspect of yourself and give it what it wants.

Since a customer is a hidden aspect of yourself, naturally, upon its discovery, you want to give him or her what they want.

Even customers who reject you (How can they be customers if they reject you?) are hidden aspects of yourself. Only they are further removed.

Creating Worries for the Movie Theater of My Mind

Do I thrive on worry?

Do I need it as a motivator?

If I had no financial worries, would I create them simply to keep myself entertained?

I am in the self-entertainment business. I entertain myself all day by creating worries and glories.

Suppose I suddenly made a lot of money, and financial worries disappeared. Would I create non-financial ones?

Evidently, I need worries. That is why I create them.

Worry is not bad, just unpleasant and annoying; sometimes it is downright frightening and terrorizing. Nevertheless, creating worry and anxiety-producing scenarios is part of the entertainment business. They keep me returning to the movie theater of my mind. I never want to miss a show.

Right now I am in the middle of the Financial Apocalypse adventure story. It is a fascinating horror show that may last years. If it ends, will a new show will take its place? It may turn out to be another horror show but one of a different nature. Some titles that come to mind are: Alzheimer Alley, Nursing Home Frenzy, I Learned To Ice Skate At Greystone Academy For The Insane,

Sliding Down Cardiac Mountain, and the police thriller Cardiac Arrest.

What can I do about these movies?

Nothing. Just watch, enjoy, and let them run their course. Eventually, a new one will come to the theater of my mind.

Pain

How to handle pain:
Go straight into it. Watch it. . . and see it dissolve.

High-Probability Selling (HPS)

Alice wrote me inquiring about my Czech tour. I called her back not to sell her but to see if I could disqualify her!

This is a new wonderful sales perspective. Alice was my first prospect. It turns out she is eighty-two years old, has traveled all over the world, is of Czech origin and has been to the Czech Republic thirteen times. My tour still interested her. Then, in an attempt to disqualify her I told her the price. (I "give answers" by asking questions. It's part of the HPS method.) She said it was more than she expected to spend. This statement immediately disqualified her.

I mailed her a brochure and itinerary anyway. I did it just in case I judged her wrong. Was I wasting my time? I don't know. But in any case, in my mind, she is out.

Two years later I still hadn't heard from her. I was right.

Guitar: Restaurant/Coffee House

Should I play guitar in a restaurant or coffee house?

What's stopping me from doing this?

First, it must pay money! That's part of the fun. How much payment? Ask $250 per night; then go to $175. Offer an evening of "trying it out." For free? For $100? Explore this. One time per week, say, Friday night.

I'm about to do this. Will I? Money will make it real; money will push me to act. Here is the real motivational meaning of money.

It's a labor of love; but it is also a labor of payment. I need both. What would come out of a restaurant/café job?

1. Reach a new audience for tours, weekends, folk dance classes, even guitar lessons.

2. "Free" advertising in a new market. Put out my brochures, display them as my "card."

3. Guitar playing satisfaction.

4. "Pure classical." But I could also throw in songs. (If I do, it's $250.) Then it would be An Evening With Jim Gold type show.

I could do one set of classical guitar, one set of songs.

Songs in a restaurant as "background." It would be good training for me to learn how to "practice singing in public" with the same "inward concentration" as classical guitar. In other words, without trying to "grab the audience."

5. It keeps my repertoire sharp and going.

6. It will promote other bookings, club dates etc.

Generally, it is a good place to practice guitar and songs in public. And get paid. On a steady (weekly) basis.

So far, on every level, it is a good idea. Let's see if it sticks.

I can also bring the restaurant itself customers by promoting the event in my folk dance classes and through ads. A join campaign. We advertise both the restaurant and myself.

From God's point of view, where I am in my development right now, is exactly where I'm supposed to be. And this is true at all times.

The Big Question

In Sook emailed me from Korea. He wanted to know all about my Folk Tours.

It made me realize not only the international potential of the internet, but the vast international potential of my tour business.

He raised a big question in my mind:

Why have I not been able to mine the vast potential of my tour business?

This may be one of the great challenges in my life. How to mine my treasures, sell my treasures, bring my treasures public—and get the public to pay for it. Paying for it means they value it!

First step: Recognize my tours as treasures.

Uncle Leon's Visit

"Uncle" Leon had the right ideas, namely, I should, could, and can expand my Folk Tour business. He saw its vast potential. Perhaps that is why he came to me: to bring me this message. He came as a messenger from God. The message he brought was the vast potential of my tour business. His only purpose was to present the message. It was not his purpose to fulfill it. He was the messenger, not the substance and material. "Uncle" Leon was not the right form.

I am the substance and material.

I am the right form.

Can I fulfill such potential? Can I continue my inner expansion, express and concretize it by selling my vision to the outside world? Do I have the ability to bring my treasures public? These are the big questions.

Let my tour business be an expression of soaring!

Flying into Rome I had the gift of three free seats next to me on the plane. Best transatlantic sleep I've ever had.

Then we flew into Palermo, met our Sicilian guide, Marco. I like him. We drove into the city and settled into our Excelsior Hotel.

I took a short walk through the main street in Palermo, past lots of clothing stores. Unimpressed, I returned to my room, took an hour sleep, and woke with the familiar tour feeling of "What am I doing here, anyway?" Why didn't I stay home where I can read the Torah, play guitar, write, study, read, run, and do yoga? Why am I here in the first place?

I often feel this way at the beginning of a tour. Perhaps I'm just tired from the jet lag.

In any case, the following day was a great one! Our local guide, Pina, short for Joseph or Guiseppi, lead us on a tour of Palermo. His talk was filled with passion. I ended up feeling bad for the Sicilians. What a history! Let's just say the Jews, Arabs, and Sicilian nobility really got it in the neck. Especially when the Jesuit Inquisition came to town under the Spanish. Such damage and destruction can last centuries, and it did with the Sicilians. But what a great culture in the middle ages! Palermo stood up as one of the most important cities in Europe, the greatest in the twelfth and thirteenth centuries under the Normans, Roger of Hauteville, King Roger II, William the Bad and William the Good, the Hohenstaufens with Henry the sixth, and finally Frederick II. His reign was called Stupor Mundi! How I love that title! It means not Stupid of the World or Stupor of the World but rather Wonder of the World.

After the 12th-century Spanish kabbalistic Rabbi Abulafia tried converting the Pope to Judaism. After that he came to Palermo where he spent five years before returning to Spain.

In the afternoon, I went to a Palermo bookstore and, after purchasing books on the Normans, History of Sicily, and the Sicilian Jews—all in Italian, of course, I saw a book on Frederick II written by, guess who? David Abulafia. Turns out he teaches history in Cambridge University in England. The book was written in English then translated into Italian. Perhaps David Abulafia is a descendant of the Abulafia family from which Rabbi Abulafia came.

Order: The "Only" Way

I overslept this morning. To my disappointment, I woke up at 5:30 instead of 4:00 a.m. I turned off my alarm, figuring I could wake up mentally. Wrong. I am still on jet lag time. In any case, after waking up late I decided to eliminate writing from my morning routine. I washed, had coffee, studied Torah in Hebrew, then began yoga. But I couldn't concentrate during my first Salute to the Sun. Writing gnawed at my brain. Finally, I took out my computer and wrote these pages.

What does this show? I must follow my routines in their proper order. If I have little time just spend less time with each routine.

The Birth Of A La Marco Tour Notes

First we visited Trapani and the Pepoli museum in northwestern Sicily, then drove 800 meters up a mountain to the medieval town of

Erice. Shrouded in fog, it gave me a truly medieval experience of cold, wet, fog, dampness, low visibility; the thrill of Hamlet lost in Denmark on a cold night. We ate local couscous, returned to the bus, drove down the mountain and back to Palermo again.

Erice was really a thrill a minute. When I got back to my room and reviewed Marco's excellent history notes, I had an idea:

Make my own a la Marco notes for future tours!

I could put years of history study and knowledge into practice, learning to verbalize it as well. I could make a la Marco notes for each country I tour, put the notes into my computer, print them out and give them to my tour participants. It would focus my tours on educating myself and, parenthetically, it might educate my tourists as well.

That's my "new" tour philosophy. No longer to make money—although that would be nice. But for inspiration, purpose, meaning, and motivation, I'd best run my tours to educate myself. What better purpose than to fill my life with joy and the glow of personal expansion. Start by writing, and publishing my history a la Marco.

Foggy Sicilian Morning

The historical significance of asteroids hurtling through space, turning machines into non-entities and waking up interstellar parlor games, flits through my mind. Must they be accounted for? How about the stellar limitations of our trip to Erice, haunting in their munificence, thrilled and perforated by a fog of narrow straits and isthmuses gone wild with herrings and baited mattanza tuna hunting breaths. Only the salvation of a Sicilian magnificence can haunt such a lair. Mental bombardments and warm-ups cannot necessarily hamper a historian whose calling smacks of chicken and odors wrapped in rooster cellophane before the barnyard fog of Trapani or Palermo.

Racing through inner tubes, turning intestines in brain fodder, wrestling with the giant questions of poet or historian. Can I take dry facts, turn them into wet noodles swimming in delicious sauce, and fit these succulent nutrients of a spaghetti fed environment into a last first supper to feed myself and my family? Is history writing just another passing dream, a momentary fantasy built over a Sicilian well of emptiness, a simple filling of new hay for a barn, a passing cloud on the horizon that evaporates as soon as this tour ends? Or is history writing a new direction?

What do I like about history?

First, and perhaps foremost, I like the explosions of lingual velocity in my mouth as I pronounce the names of ancient personages and places. Mine is a musical approach to history, a velar and stellar approach. Flying backwards over time, letting my imagination soar, sailing across the Euphrates, visiting Babylonia, seeing stars shine under Phoenician nights, quick visits to Carthage, then jump two thousand years forward to Tunisia before backtracking two and a half millenia to visit Pythagoras at his home in ancient Crotona. My Greek is rusty, especially my ancient Greek. Will Pythagoras understand me? Will we need a translator?

Will I allow history writing to come straight from my imagination?

Good unanswerable questions on this foggy Sicilian morning.

Idiots Of The World

I came to dinner last night and sat next to Doris. The first thing she said was, "I'm so mad. Why weren't our festival tickets and performances arranged beforehand? We should have gone to a performance tonight. Why did I come on this trip, anyway? You should have known about this festival program and made arrangements in advance." She said a few more things, but I got so upset I didn't hear the rest of her vitriolic barb. This idiot was criticizing my tour! What's more, she was criticizing *me!* Who does she think she is? What does she know about running a tour, anyway? Nothing, of course. But that didn't stop her. She didn't even bother asking me any questions. She simply assumed everything was all screwed up, that I wasn't doing my job, that the tour was disorganized, and that nothing good was going to happen at this festival, that she would be cheated and unhappy. So, in her atrocious manner, she blamed me for her bilious frustration.

I felt an immediate volcanic rumbling in my belly; the white-hot lava from my intestinal Mount Etna was about to erupt. But I restrained myself from strangling her,

I was about to defend myself by explaining how this tour works, but I didn't. Actually, I didn't know what to say because the beauty of my tours is that I don't quite know how they work. For example, I don't know yet what's going on at the Agrigento Festival. It's my first time here. But even if I were here for the second, third, or tenth time, I still wouldn't know what's going on. In fact, I even pride myself on not knowing what's going on. Then I seize the moment, grab the day, and find my way. Each situation calls for a different response. You really can't know exactly what to do until you're in it. Knowing what to do, working my way through the situation, handling the spur-of-the-moment decision, is not only what I like to do, but the best way to do things. Too much early planning is often as bad as too little. But why explain all this to dumphead Doris? She's just too stupid and angry to understand anything beyond her childish tantrums and imaginary creations.

I wanted to get more information about the Festival before I spoke to our group so I got up from dinner, went to a phone and called Michelle Gallo, our local tour guide. He gave me more details, which I passed on. It helped. Marge, who had picked up on Doris's discontents, chiming in with her own worries but later apologized to me for acting so childish.

I don't mind Marge, Doris, or anyone else asking for favors or even trying to effect change in our program. But I absolutely hate their demanding, pouting, asinine, assumptive manner of blame and accusation.

Now the question was how to act.

I called Michelle Gallo again and got more information. We set up a meeting with a local Sicilian folk dance group. Michelle said he would also try getting tickets to performances on Friday and Saturday night. Another tour situation saved.

Later I asked Doris, "Do you feel better?"

She answered, "Absolutely not. This should have been arranged in advance. It's your responsibility."

I hissed quietly. Then I left our hotel to take a short walk around the block and meditate upon idiots of the world.

Faultline Meets the Supreme Sparker

Thank God for Aaron. I don't mean biblical Aaron, but rather Aaron Kirchenbaum, who told me in Mykonos, that the shock I get from touching my computer comes because I'm barefoot. Current passes through me into the ground. Now when I use my computer, I wear shoes.

Yesterday, in Agrigento, we met our first Sicilian folk dance group. They performed a Tarantella, then taught us basic Tarantella steps with lots of enthusiasm. I made good dance contacts for next year. Working with our local guide, Michelle Gallo, we set up a 1999 tour program. We'll return to the Almond Festival in Agrigento next February, meet folk dance groups, visit a Sicilian village, meet the local people, and dance some more.

Finally, I had put my Sicilian tour together! I felt satisfied.

Then, as often happens after a success, I was visited by Mr. Down Faultline. He is the miserable gnome inhabiting the southern intellectual sector of my brain. He tried to kill my jubilation. "You can hardly call this a victory," he said. "You've done it so often. Putting tours together has become easy for you." Leaning on his stick, he tried making a hole in my brain. "It is also important to remember that you'll soon be dead. If not tomorrow, next week, or next year, certainly in thirty, forty, or fifty years. When doesn't matter. So why bother feeling good or bad about accomplishments? All will be forgotten. It all ends up down the drain." At first I agreed. Then I realized Faultline is right only on one level. On a higher level, he is wrong. My victories are sparks of spirit in action, bathing me in holy waters. Down Faultline, as a representative of the fragmented intellectual sector of my brain, speaks to the other fragmented sectors, exhorting them to "be reasonable." But I travel in Lands Beyond Intellect, where sparks fly. In a whirling success column of rising sparks, I ascend to meet the Supreme Sparker.

How To Prevent Sleep Walking

Later in the afternoon we arrived at Siracusa. We visited the archaeological park with an excellent local guide named Salvatore.

However, I couldn't concentrate on what he was saying. I kept falling asleep. When I didn't, I wished I were somewhere else. How boring these wonderful archeological lectures are. How amazing that such knowledgeable guides imparting such important historic and cultural information put me to sleep almost every time. What a shame I can't concentrate on what they're saying. Yet even thought I like history, I can't help it.

It has always been thus.

But maybe, by expanding through a few helpful words from Paul Kerlee, I can find a way out. Paul fell asleep at the concert last night. He said, "I always fall asleep at concerts. I also fall asleep at lectures, during classes, and sometimes even when someone talks to me. That's why I started videoing: It keeps me awake."

I liked that. I understood it. The process of videoing keeps him awake. Paul is participating in and in charge of his own creative process. He has found a personal approach to staying awake through life, a way to handles times of stress and boredom. I could do something similar.

I thought: If creativity is my God connection, then I should keep this connection at all times. Creativity wakes me up and keeps me alert. Why not use it, in the form of writing, calligraphy, drawing or whatever, while tour guides are lecturing.

How do I stay awake? Here are some answers:

1. Keep a writing pad in hand while touring. Keep it on in hand as the tour guide lectures.

2. Use free form spontaneous writing while they speak. Use their soporific lectures to "verbally take off."

Here's what came out of this approach as I used in Siracusa:

Dionysus ear: *Orrechio di Dionysus.* Siracuse. *Cir-a-kus-a.* Cir-excuse. Slaves slaving, carving out today's paradise. Romans, Greeks. Read Thucydides. Thoo-sid-a-dees. Write Thucydides using Greek letters.

Write by hand. A free writing hand. Thus can I jump, writing many alphabets. Learn calligraphy. Write in Hebrew, Cyrillic, Greek, and Arabic alphabets.

Carry different pens on my person at all times.

Tombs of the acropolis, lava of Mount Etna, marine bodies stuck on the back of ancient graves. *J'ai rencontre un homme de Bordeaux.*

Eonus led the first slave rebellion on Sicily against Rome around 129 A.D. Spartacus was about 73 A.D.

They Can Hurt You

At a gut level, there is something about Marge that frightens me. After she exploded in Agrigento when the festival scheduling didn't go exactly her way, I realized why my instincts were right. Although quiet and restrained on the outside, inside she is a volcano about to erupt. She explodes when things don't go her way.

I am right to be afraid of her. She can give me a very hard time. She could potentially ruin my tour. I try to be friendly when I talk to her, hoping to keep her volcano from exploding. Who needs the trouble she can create? Certainly not I. Therefore, it is wise that I use my wiles to calm her. Potential loose cannons must have their powder checked. If charm, friendliness, and wit will keep her in place, so much the better. It is wise to fear some folks. They can hurt you.

Nightmare

It's our last day in Sicily. Soon we'll drive to the Catania airport and fly to Rome.

I awoke this morning after a nightmare. Our group attended a concert. At the end, we, along with the entire audience left the theater hall, went outside, and were attacked by a group of Sicilian gansters. Somehow I was the leader in our counter attack. My only weapon was a stick and some kind of hidden crazy courage. I waved it wildly, threatening them as I do the dogs that bark at me along my running route. It seemed to work. They didn't hit or kill any of us. But they continued shouting and threatening us. Then I awoke.

What does this dream mean? Could it signal a new confidence, an ability to gesticulate wildly against the dogs of fear, and thus protect myself and my group? What threat do these Sicilian gansters represent? The threat of our upcoming Roman extension?

Good questions on my last morning in Sicily.

Improving

We arrived in Rome yesterday. I have a lovely room at the Universeo Hotel.

I'm sorry now I booked Pompeii. Should I go? Or take advantage of this beautiful room, walk around the city, take a rest, and visit Pompeii next year? Visiting it next year would give me something to look forward to. In my heart, I'd like to do that. But I have a group to consider. How disappointed will it be to them if I don't go? On the other hand, how disappointed will it be to me if I do go? Ever the conflict. At the moment, I'm leaning towards going. We'll see. . . .

Enthusiasm

Enthusiasm through love of languages, history, and culture, is the best way to sell my tours. It is the connection between study, sales, love of learning, and business.

Enthusiasm, rather than fear of poverty and financial destruction, is my best sales tool.

Weekends

Ruth asked: "How did you get so many people on this Folk Dance Weekend?"

"God gets the credit," I answered.

But God is within.

So I get the credit, too.

Return to the Baltics

Lithuania, Latvia, and Estonia touch my heart. Their music is pleasant and moderate, their folk dancing pleasant and moderate, their folk costumes pleasant and moderate; the people are handsome, beautiful. . .and pleasant and moderate. Our Lithuanian guide, Eimute, although somewhat stiff, was pleasant and moderate; our Estonian guide, Endrik, is closed off, but with a fine sense of humor. Best so far has been Aija, our Latvian guide. I'd come back to Latvia in 2001 for the Riga Festival simply for her to guide us, Other highlight of our Baltic tour were the patterns and designs on the Estonian sweaters. The beautiful Tallinn handicrafts gave me a sparking moment.

I am looking for a personal reason to return to the Baltics. Did I miss something here? What is hidden within these cultures that I do not see? So far, except for that brief Estonian sweater-design moment of inspiration, I haven't found the necessary spark to return.

Finland now looks interesting. If I travel to Finland, why not add Sweden and Norway—and even Iceland. A Scandinavian tour for 2000? We'll see.

This tour has been beautifully run. Union Tours is a fine company. It has lots of class, and so does its president, Stephanie Horton. I'm working with good people here. That in itself is a big plus.

Strangely, I feel a certain dullness in these cultures of moderation and calm. And this despite the incredible pageantry of the Estonian Folk Festival; its largeness overwhelmed me. It is hard to "get personal" with eight thousand dancers dancing in a football stadium. Nonetheless, seeing thousands participating, whether dancing on a football field or singing in an outdoor theater, has its own special meaning. I don't know what to make of it. I'd like to like it, but so far it has not touched my soul.

How excited can you get about reasonable, practical, or organizational things, anyway? I've always considered them first steps in preparing oneself for the magical spark that illuminates life in one crashing, dynamic, brilliant, serendipitous mystical moment. Yet there is a strong practical and reasonable part of me. I am a good organizer, too. So good, in fact, that I hardly ever give it a second thought. From finding my way in a strange town to straightening up a messy room, I have a natural inner organizing ability. It is simply one of those faculties that comes easily like singing and ad libbing during my concerts. I hardly pay attention to it since it is so easy. Rather I focus on improving my classical guitar which is so hard.

Is my Baltic tour experience a subtle reminder I have put my organizing talents, along with my practical and reasonable side, in second place? What away to look at it! Learning to appreciate these qualities might contain the "deeper mystical meaning" of why I ran this tour in the first place. It would certainly make it meaningful. It might even give me a reason to return to the Baltics.

Needed: A Fresh Vision Of Russia

I feel disappointed this morning. And this after visiting the Hermitage yesterday, then seeing a fabulous Russian folk group, the Volga People's Chorus, from Samara.

They were simply sensational—a la Moiseyev. And yet something in me keeps saying "I've been through all this before." The edge is off. I'm somewhere else.

Where?

I'm looking for a new idea to inspire me.

Technically, this continues to be a great tour. Our guide, Antonina, is excellent. A real plus.

This searching problem is within myself. I'm ready to explore a new level. My old views of Russia, tourism, travel, and the travel business are dead. I need new reasons for visiting St. Petersburg. I sit at my window in the St. Petersburg hotel overlooking the Neva River thinking: Time for Russian rebirth.

I am resisting Russia. Part of me is living in pre-conceived notions. This has been true for most of this tour. First, in the Baltic countries of Lithuania, Latvia, and Estonia, I kept thinking they were Bulgaria and comparing the music and dance to Bulgarian music and dance. But of course, they are different. I only "realized" this in my heart on the ninth day of the tour.

Living in the past with its pre-conceived notions is also happening to me in St. Petersburg. I have past notions of 1987, meeting with Moiseyev and his dance company, walking the streets of Leningrad, thrilling to Russian music, language learning, and dance, and to the fight for survival in handling the communist "Nyet, nyet" bureaucracy so well.

I was fired with newness, learning, and fear.

Now these feelings are all gone.

Where do I go from here?

We'll see where this leads.

Our first day in Slovakia:

Upon arrival in Kosice, this capital of Eastern Slovakia appeared like a shithole lost in nuclear waste. And this, coupled with my afternoon walk down a desolate Kosice street brought up my usual first-day tour question: "Why am I here?"

But on second viewing, great inner beauty appeared.

Our meeting at the airport with Jan Pumpr of Dvorana, the Czech agency of Jitka Bonusova with whom I work, and Jan's serendipitous meeting with a folk dance friend in our Centrum Hotel lobby, followed by an invitation to a rehearsal of the Jahodna Slovak folk dance troupe, made our first evening in Slovakia a smash hit.

What a night! Another miracle manufactured out of nothing. Our exhausted dancers returned to their hotel rooms with smiles on their sleepy, hollow-eyed, jet-lagged faces.

How can I not return to the Czech Republic and Slovakia next year? I have such excellent contacts, itinerary, and events. This tour is a true winner. The only problem is, as usual, how to get customers to fill the bus traveling through this beautiful program.

Shouldn't all my dancers come on this incredible tour? Indeed, they should. It should be required for every folk dancers. How can they dance if they have not had this life-changing tour experience? Without it their vision and folk dancing remain shallow and superficial.

How do I communicate my enthusiasm and transmit the mystical beauty of these tours?

I don't know... yet.

As I sat in the amphitheater in Helpa watching the folk dancers and singers from central Slovakia including the fabulous group from East Slovakia, Zeleziar, many polyphonic, multifaceted thoughts and directions came to mind:

1. Languages! If I want to find a reason to run tours, an inspiration that will last all year long and for many years to come, I must return to learning languages. They are my central core of study and inspiration. I realized it again when I bought my Slovakia T-shirts from a Hungarian in Helpa. First, he spoke to me in Slovak. Then, when he saw how I could not understand him he asked if I spoke

German or Hungarian. I answered "Igen" (Yes in Hungarian.) As I dug out old quasi-forgotten words from the antiquated computer memory of my former Hungarian brain, I formed them on my lips and remembered the pleasure I always felt speaking the marvelous magyar tongue so full of paprikash and fire.

Learning and practicing languages on the local population has always been one of my great touring pleasures. Hungarian, Czech, Slovak, Bulgarian, Russian, Greek, Turkish, Arabic, Hebrew, Italian, French, Spanish, Portuguese, even Georgian and Armenia—I've tried them all. True, I can't speak any of them well. But who cares? I love them. They inspire me. That's enough.

2. My tours must go where the folklore is alive! After all, they are folk tours. Folklore, especially folk dance, is what I love. Eastern Europe has the most developed and sophisticated folklore. It is alive and hidden in little unknown countries like Bulgaria, Slovakia, the back woods of Bohemia and Moravia, Romania, or along the less traveled paths of "known" countries like Greece, Turkey, Israel, Italy, and more.

Some new thoughts:

I've spent thousands of dollars and many years of travel to find the correct spelling and meaning of the folk dance from the Slovak village of Helpa that we, in America, call "Horehronsky Cardas." Slovaks call it "To Ta Helpa." *Hore* means "up" or "upper"; Hron is the name of a river; *sky* is an adjectival ending for a masculine noun. Thus, "Horehronsky Cardas." Write an inverted carrot or *hacek* over the *c* and *s* in *cardas*. Horehronsky carda means csardas from the upper Hron. Lower Hron would be called "dolny Hron."

Also the sign on my T-shirt: "Horehronske Oslavy" means Horehronske—adjectival form for a plural ending; *oslavy*—east (a "singular" noun that uses a plural form).

Rewards!

We're leaving for the Prague airport in a few hours.

I feel sad. Anxious, too. What will my "new life" in America bring?

Yesterday I was hit by the old travel anxiety block-buster. It's the

"I hate to leave the safe haven of home" feeling. Over the past two weeks Slovakia and the Czech Republic have become my home. After the initial arrival in Kosice I settled in. Slowly jet lag ended. The tour came together. I became comfortable with our problems and lack of problems. Gabriela guided us. Vladimir drove us. Jitka designed a fine program. I oversaw it all. I was in charge, watching, making sure tour plans were carried out. I bore the weight of responsibility on both a conscious and unconscious level. It lessened slightly as the tour came together, but, in reality, it never ended, even during the last two days when my tourists had free time. Though on the surface it may have looked like I was doing nothing, I was doing mucho. Only my work was invisible. The outsider might see an easy going tour leader enjoying himself on his tour. The insider would see a never-ending thought process going on inside my brain. Motion, growth, decisions, future plans, birth of new ideas. This inner movement, later reflected in outer movement, is called work!

I am constantly working.

Running a tour is an honor, privilege, pain, and a glory.

These glorious, jagged, melt-down feeling are my rewards.

I'm off to America.

Before our flight to Ioannina at the Athens airport a Greek woman said: "When Greeks dance, we look at the face and heart, not the feet."

Tsamikos mood: "I want to live! But nevertheless, I am going out to die for my freedom.

"Attract people to the best in yourself."
—Joan

Misery Just Doesn t Work its Old Magic Anymore

I used to be a good angry writer. Rage could rumble my stomach, squeeze my pancreas, ignite my intestine. And if not rage, at least depression. I was good at it. Ah, depression. What a turn on. The sliding descent into the lowlands and from there into the bottomless valleys of scum, slime, noxious fumes with rivers of garbage flowing all around me used to somehow thrill my porcupine-punctured being in a down-swirling whirlwind of self-disgust, sadness, and pity. I used to "enjoy" wallowing in all that rich mud, the good dirt of self-burial preceded by a few tasty beatings with the whip of self-flagellation.

But these transient pleasures seem to have fled. Certainly, they have lost their bite. And this mainly because I don't believe them anymore. Sure, last night's folk dance felt like shit. Hardly anyone showed up. The ones who did were decrepit dancers who could hardly move. A few lively ones came later but by then it was too late. But the strange thing about all this was that I enjoy teaching these miserable dancers. I enjoyed seeing their smiling faces even as their slow-moving, inexperienced feet stumble in all directions. I enjoy working with such a group of aging bodies, and this because even though only a few show up, they are, nevertheless, a group of souls. I enjoy teaching souls. Can I help it if they are encased in decrepit bodies? Is it their fault they are old, arthritic, falling apart, can't move fast—or even slowly for that matter? Part of me doesn't care. Deep in my heart, I realize sometimes God sends me large crowds, small groups, and sometimes He sends me a vacuum. But I even enjoy teaching when no one shows up. After all, I can always teach myself. That's who I'm teaching anyway even if there is a crowd. On the deepest level, who are my students anyway but an extension of me.

But this is all philosophy. Truth is, self-misery has lost its stranglehold and power over me. I don't know what I'll do for entertainment from now on.

Am I At The End Of My Career?

Am I at the end of my career?

Are folk dance classes, weekends, and tours coming to an end?

And this not because business stinks—which it does. But rather because something internal is happening to me.

I am not frightened by this change, just puzzled.

Sure I'm upset that business is so dead. No matter how many announcements I make about parties, New Years Weekend, or tours, I get no response. Dead eyes all around. Discouraging, indeed. But

I've been through this kind of discouragement before. In the past, when I reached bottom, I'd always say, "Never! I'll never give up."

But now I think, if my business is going to die, let it die. I'll do something else.

I went through a career change about twenty years ago, gradually gave up my guitar concert career, and started teaching folk dancing, running weekends and tours. So there is a precedent.

Now the folk dance business seems dead. But does this deadness really exist? Or is it only inside my mind? Do I actually want to end my career? Or look at it differently?

I hate the constant worry about registration, class attendance, and all the other business and financial fears that beset the solo entrepreneur. Some say worries go with the territory. Do they? Can't I live in the territory and not worry? Who says I have to worry? Why not simply learn to take what comes, focus on the present, whether it be only three students in a folk dance class, four on a weekend or five on a tour? This is territory too. It is I who have decided to worry about who and how many register. I'm giving that up. Time to move on.

That is what I mean by "I'm at the end of my career."

But I'm also excited about giving it up. Imagine, starting over. It is so freeing, full of hope.

What is the first mad, insane, crazy, outrageous thing that comes to mind when I think about starting a new career? Writing!

Sell my writing! Outrageous, indeed. Making money writing is even more difficult than making money playing guitar, teaching folk dancing, or running tours and weekends. Especially if I sell only my own writing.

This idea is so impossibly insane that I absolutely love it!

It could be my new direction.

I'm not leaving my folk dance, weekend, and tour businesses right away. But I will look at this mosaic differently.

Fun and Play Emerge Victorious!

Business as fun? Sales, calling, mailing, advertising, PR, as fun? These concepts are utterly foreign to me.

Yet the only way I want to go back into business is with a fun attitude.

I believe in fun and play. They are basic values—and conquests. If I can play and have fun, it means I have conquered my fears in that area. I roar out my victory cry. Playfully, I romp on the prairies, cavorting, racing, jumping, a wild horse having a great time.

This is ultimate victory! To stand triumphant and shout a screaming, yap-yelping yes!

Blast away put-downs. Rip wet blankets to shreds. Lids are off! Power is up! I win. Fun and play emerge victorious.

This direction is filled with meaningless purpose and purposeless meaning.

The sophisticated words for fun and play are "artistic" and "creative."

In adult terms, a fun person means an artistic person.

A playful person means a creative person.

That's why artists and creative people have been such heroes to me. They retain fun and wonder, live a childlike life, and play at the edge of the abyss.

Ad Agency

1. Write my own ads. Crazy ads. Wild, wooly, enthusiastic ads. Then start my own ad agency!

Ads, promotion, and public relations, are fields I've always hated with a passion. This means I have a passion for it even thought that passion expressed through hatred. The key word here is passion.

Passionate hatred means I have a passionate attraction to the hated object. Opposites attract and are often the "same." My hatred can thus "easily" turn into love. (I once hated the stock market and look how I fell in love with it.)

2. I can use start by using my writing and artistic skills to create my own brochures. Rather than hire Barbara, use her as a consultant, teacher, guide, and helper.

For this I have to learn more computer and graphic art skills. I may even learn to create my own web pages. . . but that is farther down the line.

Become A Walking Ad Agency

This Ad Agency approach would also be expressed in my concert and folk dance bookings. These are really sales programs in disguise. They promote my events.

Become a walking Ad Agency. Go public in a large way.

Mystic Knowledge

Personal experience is the mystic's road. That's why people should go to the Koprivshtitsa Folk Festival in Bulgaria. There they can gain experiential knowledge of Bulgarian customs, history, folklore, arts, language, and people.

I offer the possibility of receiving mystic knowledge on my tours. All other knowledge is, at best, intellectual, at worst, poppycock.

Should I Bring My Computer to Tunisia?

I thought I was "cured" of my incessant desire to write. The haunting voice had been silenced and I could have some inner peace. But instead, the opposite is true. The inner voice is not silenced, but, if I don't write, it keeps getting louder! The only way to get rid of it, to "shut it up," is to ex-press it through writing.

Evidently, like sex, hunger, and desire for adventure, I will never be free of this voice. It will haunt me, not only until I die, but also after death in the next life, and the next, too. Certainly, it is part of being in the ring. I have chosen to fight in the ring rather than stay on the sidelines observing. This paradoxical, wonderful, miserable, illuminating, and bothersome daily writing is just another part of that daily struggle. That's why I must bring my computer to Tunisia, even though carrying it, and relearning its WP5 program, is such a pain in the ass. Choosing not to bring it means I have chosen to remain on the writing sidelines. Sure, I rationalize it's only two weeks away, it's a pain bringing it, and I'll only use it two or three times, anyway. Why bother? Well, those two or three times may be worth the entire trip. Plus, isn't there the symbolic value of bringing it? And this, even if I do nothing with it. Carrying the computer "on my person," lugging it with me on bus and plane and from one hotel to the next means I am still in the fight.

Cosmic Purposes of my Tourists

Connie loved *Crusader Tours* and "Rebirth in a Major Key." I reread it. I loved it, too! Great sense of humor and philosophy. I agree with it completely.

I love my writing best.

Rereading the goodness of *Crusader Tours* will remind and motivate me to publish *New Leaf*.

The cosmic purpose of this Tunisian tour is:

1. See my inner tour self in action. That's why Marilyn and Joan on this tour: to teach, test, show, and demonstrate this to me.

2. To realize I must publish *New Leaf*.

Connie came on this trip to reveal the value of *Crusader Tours* to me.

Joan came to help me practice growth and expansion among the weeds, and strengthen me in dealing with the world at large.

Isn't is strange Connie and Joan argued with each other? They signified opposites struggling within me. Connie represents looseness and flexibility; Joan represents compulsion, and order.

Both are necessary.

People like Marilyn and Joan are good for the group. They are sent my God, inshallah (If God wills it) to teach me how to deal with them, handle myself, and grow in the process.

I should open my tours up to anybody. (Not the Jim R. types, of course. I'm not asking for suicide.)

Thank you Joan and Marilyn. Your minuses have turned into pluses. I see enthusiasms in negativity. I view both sides, and am calm.

So many concepts of self and attitudes have coalesced on this tour. No wonder I have a slight headache. But, bottom line is, I can't stand the glory and magnificence of such wonderful personal changes. Holding back my excitement is giving me a headache.

I am not facing the wonderful job I have done. But now I will.

Get excited! Explode! Revel in the glory of running this tour! It's a sure cure for this headache.

Miracle: The Dows got their standby flight to Paris largely because I encouraged them. I said, "Don't discount the miracle factor. Give it your best shot. Expect nothing. Pray for a miracle."
It happened!

All Is One: The Whole Room Got Up to Dance!

I taught dancing at the Tessler Bat Mitzvah in Madison, Connecticut. I worried: Will people get up to dance? I'm walking at the edge of humiliation. If they don't get up, no one dances, I'll have to accept payment for, ostensibly, "doing nothing." This is my ego's biggest fear. When I work at a Bat Mitzvah or any event, I am vulnerable, and at the mercy of the crowd's wishes. And they may wish not to dance.

Here's what happened: After much hidden trepidation (I know it was "hidden" because I ended up hurting my back when I bent slightly over to pick up my guitar) I walked to the center of the room. Everyone was eating lunch. I announced "Good afternoon, everyone. Welcome to the Emma Tessler Bat Mitzvah. Now we are going to learn the hora and how to dance Israeli dancing." This announcement was greeted by absolute silence and total indifference. People continued eating as if I had said nothing. They talked, chattered, bantered with one another. Embarrassing to me, indeed. How would I get them to do anything? I figure I'd better go over to each table and ask them personally if anyone wanted to dance. When I did, a few smiling heads nodded and some smiling faces said yes. I looked back at the dance floor and, lo and behold, three people were standing there. Evidently, they had heeded my announcement.

Now at least I had enough dancers to start. I took the microphone, went to the center of the room, and made a second announcement. "We're starting our Israeli dancing now. You're all invited to join us!" Then, to my utter amazement the whole room got up! One hundred people pushed their seats back, rose, and soon mobbed the dance floor! Quickly I changed my starting plan from an improvised Klezmer circle walking improvisation to the Israeli dance Zemer Atik. I told everyone to form first two, then three circles. In three circles no one can see my steps. I realized immediately that teaching dance steps to this beginner crowd would be impossible in the absence of watching my feet. I'd decided to teach these dancers with my hands! I raised them high above my head and, through gestures, nods, finger pointing, and moving my arms about, I guided them through Zemer Atik. It worked beautifully. They hooted, screamed, hollered, and laughed as they flopped and slopped through the dance. After four or five repetitions it actually began to look good! They all cheered at the end. They were ecstatic. So was I. After that a flood of incredible enthusiasm was released, they lifted the bat mitzvah girl on a chair and danced wildly around her. Family and friends came forward and invented their own dance improvisations. These people were wild and crazy. . . just what I love! Thus, on first glimpse, what appeared to be a group of stiff, suited, tightly dressed, dead-head luggards turned out to be a mad, crazy, wild, enthusiastic collection of creative souls! My initial reading of them was wrong. It had been based solely on my fears.

So, with a little help from God, the afternoon dancing turned out to be an incredible success!

Later I thought: What a beautiful magical event! How can I now accept that I was responsible for creating it?

Then I realized I was not alone. Obviously, I could not have done it without the bat mitzvah participants and the help of God. He created the ultimate miracle of our togetherness.

I can write, play guitar, run, do yoga, study, and follow my miracle schedule alone, but I cannot teach dancing alone. (Or do business, either.) I cannot exist without the other.

On the deepest mystical level, there are no real divisions. We are all connected. All is One. Beauty-filled, beauty-full. Beauty is the All-Is-One experience.

Now this is something to meditate on! Mediate on the beauty of folk dancing Bat Mitzvah Oneness.

Spiritual Practice

Can marketing, advertising, and promotion be spiritual practices? Was St. Paul performing a spiritual practice when he brought the gospel to others in the ancient world? The sales, marketing, and promotion of Christianity. Of course, he didn't consider it in those terms. He called it "bringing the good news."

Is "bringing the good news" a spiritual practice?

Would bringing others my writing and guitar playing qualify as good news? If it does, would I get any satisfaction, joy, fun, fulfillment performing such a task? Would it put me closer to God? Can business, the selling of my work, publishing, or giving concerts, do anything positive for my brain?

These are old questions. And, as usual, I have no answers. But maybe just the questions are enough. They are subtle reminders of the eternal question: How to cross the bridge between myself and others.

Going Without a Project

I'm leading a tour to Bulgaria without a personal project.

Maybe I'll feel differently once I get there, but for now, even the study of the Bulgarian language does not seem enough. I envision two weeks of blank mental space ahead of me.

My body aches. I am so tired. Pre-tour anxieties? Maybe. But as I look deep within myself, I cannot find any reason to be anxious about this trip. Only the habit of pre-tour anxiety is gnawing at my mind. I have lots of old "pre" anxieties: pre-concert, pre-dance class teaching, pre-weekend anxieties. But, the more I look at them, the more they fall away and fade into a calm, cloudless sky.

Am I really becoming so "laid back?" Is it an expression of self-confidence? Reflecting upon it, I can find no other answer but "yes."

It feels strange. But no matter how hard I try, I can't work up a good anxiety about this Bulgarian tour. Of course I've done all the necessary pre-tour preparation work, make name lists, collected vouchers, packed my passport, money, clothing, presents, books, and made last minute arrangements. This is all standard pre-tour stuff. But where, among these preparations, is the anxiety? It is non-existent. I am simply sailing along, calmly doing what is necessary.

Will this state of inner peace continue? Stay tuned to find out.

Calling Up the Energy

"What's the matter? people ask. "Why are you nervous? Can I help you?"

Nervousness is often seen as a negative that must be cured. But when you are excited, others never ask "What's the matter? Why are you excited? Can I help you?"

Excitement is seen as a positive state. Only happy, cured people exist in it.

I'm still nervous before my tour. I examined this feeling with the space ship of my mind, and concluded that, on the deepest level, nervousness and excitement are the same thing. They are twin forms of energy. "Nervousness" is simply the way this energy feels when you call up.

Everything I can do is done for my tour. There's nothing left to do. . . except worry. But why worry? I can't think of anything left to worry about. Yet I still do. There must be a reason for this.

I need an extraordinary amount of energy to run a tour. I am in the process of calling up my energy. Whether I use negative words like "nervousness" and "worry," or a positive word like "excitement," it is still the same energy. I am mobilizing my inner army, calling my cells, drafting atoms, molecules, neurons, sinews, and other powerful invisible cosmic elements that have slept in my body for days, months, years, eons. My nervousness is, in reality, a recruitment process. It is uncomfortable because I am not used to so much energy traveling through my system.

Sandanski, Bulgaria

I have a headache. My coffee pot has broken, exposing my morning coffee addiction.

I took Nescafe packets from the breakfast table. Perhaps they will help. I can make them with hot water from the faucet.

How will I function without coffee? I'm in a panic, and mad, too. How dependant I am on this drug for morning happiness!

In the long run, going cold turkey would be good for me.

Meanwhile the tour is going well.

Our guide, Nevena, is kind hearted, smart, sensitive, and lovely. Our folk dance teachers, Tedi and Emil, are sweet and excellent. Christo, too. Gene is starting to shine as a dancer. All good things to help the tour run smoothly.

Beyond that is my never-ending glow of confidence. Through bad or good times, it does not leave me. True, I was rattled by the late dinner service at Bansko. But even though I was baffled, tongue-tied , and startled, and, for a long moment, did not know what to do, I was "rescued" by the supportive comments of Roger, Elizabeth, Val, and Nina, and even quiet Ernesto. They said all we can do is be polite and wait for our food. This was a wonderful "obvious" answer. What I especially liked was the "be polite" part. And this out of Roger! It shows the sensitive soul behind his mask. Then Gene, Liz, Val, and Nina added supportive comments of their own, showing the largeness of their souls. Our guide, Nevena, was almost crying with frustration.

I like this largeness-of-soul approach. It is the best way.

Also, I like the way I distracted others from bad-mouthing Roger because he is so "cheap." Although he claims to be a millionaire he never has any money or wants to pay for anything. When he does, the money trickles out slowly. In any case, not only did I deflect his potential embarrassment by showing my coin tricks, I was able to admit my inner goodness to others and to myself. This melted me down and made me cry with happiness.

I am going public with inner goodness. Along with jealousy, animal growls, and the beast in me. it helped to make a wonderful day.

Love Is the Reason

I'm not angry. Rather, I'm shocked, stunned, amazed, awe-and-wondered. What a reaction to a "nothing" question: Should we bring Emil and Tedi to the Black Sea Coast?

One of the most amazing things about this onslaught from some tour members is how, on one level, it doesn't affect me. The best part of my mind is somewhere else, in another world, on another level. This has been true throughout the entire tour. That's why I can't take the complaints and frustrations between people seriously. They are, after all, only part of the reason I organize these tours.

The main reason I organize them for love. Love of dancing, love of music, language, history, and culture. And love of the people who join me. Bulgarians and my tourists. I love my tourists. But this love has little to nothing to do with the bickering, hassles, and dynamics of group relations. Dealing with them is a challenge, moving from wonderful to painful, from amusement to annoyance. But, bottom line, although relations are definitely something to be handled, they are not my main reason for coming to Bulgaria.

Love is the reason!

Everything else is a footnote, a parenthesis, a distraction that often must be dealt with so it doesn't get in the way of my prime purpose. The surface waters of the lake must be kept calm. We don't want too many waves. Keep the waters clear. Why? So you can peer down through them, see the bottom, and remember the infinite love emanating from the center.

Later: I want to get away from everyone; I need to be alone. It's nothing more than total physical exhaustion. I need to get some sleep, and a few quiet moments to think and restore myself.

I love the tour business. It's just hard to remember love when you're so tired you can hardly stand up.

It's a cold, clear, beautiful morning at Koprivshtitsa. I haven't felt cold for a week. What a nice feeling.

My room is right on main street. Very noisy. Will I ever be able to sleep in this location?

Nevertheless, I love this cool mountain air wafting through my window!

You can't be courageous if you don't have a fear to conquer.

Slights from my group are raining down on me. Well, the more the better! Bring them on! Slights are a good test of psychological strength. They throw me into a maelstrom, the nauseating, enraging whirlpool of jealousy, envy, competition, and betrayal.

Varna and the Black Sea Coast

My Bulgarian flier included a meal at the Black Sea. But my contract agreement with Renaissance Tours did not. My mistake. I will have to pay for the meal out of pocket. Lots of money going out. Nevertheless, I decided to pay for the group dinner.

I finalized the meal payment with Christo.

Then I was flooded with happiness and pride. Pride in my word! By sticking to what I promised in my flier, even at a financial loss, I am now a hero in my own eyes! It's worth all the money I pay for it.

Yes!

Yes! to wonder! Yes! to "I did it!" Yes! to stand up and be proud.

Pride in keeping my word. What a wonderful feeling!

The Pride and Joy of Accomplishment

I can usually face how bad it feels when I get things wrong. It haunts me. I cannot rest until I get it right.

But I rarely face and accept how good it feels when I get things right! Incredible pride and joy follows.

Learning to live in the pride and joy of accomplishment.

Fire of pride, river of joy. Personal accomplishment is a thrill I rarely "given in to." It used to give me a headache. Pride and joy were "too much." I would then reversed them, turn their positive energies into negatives and then turned the negatives against myself. This dampened my enthusiasm and enabled me to stay calm as flames of joy, passion, ecstasy, and bliss licked my body and mind. I was then "comfortable" in this victorious position.

But I no longer feel this way. Pride and joy in personal accomplishment are expressions of my inner room going public. I can say Yes!

Restraining this feeling of pride and joy is the main ingredient that has held me back. True, it was once "useful" in my mental fight for survival. But now it has outlived its usefulness. I no longer need it. I am moving beyond its gates into the public arena. And it feels great!

Mitzvahs

Are there any mitzvahs I perform for my group?

How do I keep my mind's eye on pride, joy, accomplishments, and the good things of this world when I am mired in the mud of transient annoyances? How can I remember my God connection when most of my body and mind are submerged in mental sewage?

Answer: Deal with tour details. Immerse myself in them. This will tie me to the immediate present. It will take my mind off the floating miseries of the limbo state.

After all, it is my mind that creates the negativity.

What is the best way to deal with it?

Ask myself if there any mitzvahs I can perform for my tour group.

Night of Folk Dancing in Darien

Do my feet hurt so much from last night's folk dancing at Darien because it was so successful. We had the best attendance ever!

In fact, could pains in my feet after folk dance class be related to my mind's attempt to dampen my enthusiasm?

Hilma stopped her $3,460 check after I purchased her ticket and land fare. I took a chance on her. This puts me $3,460 in the hole. Sure, she went to Puerto Rico to get her birth certificate. She may get her passport and even decide to join our tour after all. But... she may not. If that happens, and it may happen, I'll be stuck with a huge expense and I'll have to work mucho hard to get my money back. I may not get any of it back. I can sue her for her cancellation. But no matter what I do, this adds up to a big pain in the ass. A major annoyance.

Nevertheless, why should I let it disturb my inner peace? Let it go as just another annoyance in the sea of tours annoyances that always exist.

The hell with annoyances. Let them rain down on me, and wash off, too, like water off an umbrella. Sure, I have to handle them. But I don't have to let them pollute and destroy my mind.

I want to forget about Hilma. I laid out so much money for her tour. I am helpless to get it back. All I can do is threaten to sue her. I'll call my lawyer Bob to see if I can, but I doubt if I have a case. Even if I do, it is so much trouble.... Yet, the unfairness of it keeps gnawing at me. First consult Bob, see what options I have. If I can't sue her, I'll console myself with "learning an expensive lesson." Never trust others until I have their money! And, when rushed, always have them wire it to my bank!

Why can't I get my money back now? My father would have said: "You've learned your lesson now, Jimmy boy. Now that you finally understand, I'll take you out for ice cream."

I doubt Hilma will take me out for an ice cream refund. Even though there's little I can do about it, I'm still furious with her. I may have to satisfy myself by simply shooting her in my dreams.

Folk Dance Soring and Soaring

In "The Book of Folque Danc" by Pepe the Short, Dance Master to Louis the Half, King of France (926-934) and Emperor of the Provencal Kingdom of Half Louie, Pepe claims: "Folk dance soring leads to folk dance soaring."

Spain

Our arrival in Malaga initiated the adventure. "Malaguena," both song and dance, comes from Malaga! So does Malaguena Salerosa. It means "Salty one from Malaga." Picasso was born in Malaga.

Our group landed in Malaga. From the airport, we hopped in our tour bus driven by Jesus. Later I found out that the nickname for Jose (Joseph) is Pepe. Thus "Pepe Romero" is "Jose Romero" is "Joseph

Romero." There is also a nickname for Jesus, but I don't know what it is.

I met our guide on the domestic plane ride from Madrid to Malaga. Her name is Maite Jurado. Maite is short for Mary Teresa. She is tall, thin, and a Basque! I have never met a Basque before, except, of course, for Jorge Caneda, the organizer and prime mover of this tour. Mayte spent three days "dry-running" this tour. She visited every restaurant and hotel plus did research on dance groups we are visiting. She has a degree in architecture. Her father, Paco, an ex-engineer with IBM, now works in tourism, too. In fact, he often works with Alejandro Muniz, the director of the agency that is organizing the land arrangements for our tour through Jorge.

Anyway, after losing all of our baggage in Madrid, we hopped in our bus and headed through lovely coast, then up into exciting Serrania de Ronda mountains to Ronda, one of the lovely white towns of Andalusia. We stayed overnight in a pleasant hotel, ate supper, and fell promptly into a deep sleep.

We also had our first dance class. Fantastic! It started with a short performance of a fandango, tanguillo, sevillanas, and an improvised, or rather, choreographed version of a local dance. This was followed by a dance lesson. We learned the basic step of Sevillanas, a dance in three quarter time from Seville. We did the three-quarter time footwork and the movements of the hands. Most of us bought castanets after our teacher taught us how to use them.

Thus ended day one.

Day two we headed for Jerez de la Frontera, again driving through beautiful mountains, passing Arco de la Frontera and Jerez, the sherry capital. It is also home of Bulerias; Alegrias, however, comes from Cadiz. I love these dances and have been playing them on my guitar for years. I found out their place of origin from the waiter at our supper in Santa Puerto de Santa Maria, where our beautiful Monastery Hotel (a former monastery) is located. The waiter said his brother-in-law was the second most famous flamenco guitarist in Spain (after Paco de Lucia). He danced a few steps for us but got very shy after we demonstrated our one-day-old knowledge of the Sevillana we learned in Ronda.

Seville

We arrive in Seville. I so looked forward to my beautiful hotel room. Ah, the wonderful rug on which to do yoga, the spacious desk upon which I could place my computer and write with tranquility and inspiration, the strong, clear lighting under which I could dwell in peace, harmony, and floating mental freedom. Instead, we ended up in a real shithole far outside of the city center. My room has no rug, little space, no paintings, no decor, and no desk. We're here for three days. I felt so disappointed, especially after the beautiful Monastery Hotel rooms we had in Puerto de Santa Maria.

My room faces a narrow, noisy street with mucho motor cycles and motor-scooter noises. People talk endlessly into the night while shithole dogs bark.

But at least the hotel is clean. All the mice have taken baths, and most of the cockroaches speak Spanish. The gypsies camped outside my window are lighting fires in the building opposite me. Many play flamencan guitar. All dance Bulerias, Sevillanas, and even Alegrias. I think I see my old guitar teacher here, along with his flamencan-playing, Spanish speaking buddies.

Upon arrival, we explored Seville. The high finances of the Turkish empire were no match for our Macarena touring crew. We went to work. Joe, our Pepe, led us by taking a hammer from the back of the bus and smashing the Giraldo Tower. Soon we had torn down this masterpiece of 12th-century Almohad architecture. Although it was constructed during between 1147 and 1212, no one seemed to mind. But we did care that the Roman emperors, Hadrian, Trajan, and perhaps even Theodosius were born just outside of Seville in the now destroyed Roman town of Italica. Our purpose then was, basically, to tear down the whole city and turn it into a modern day ruin just like Italica. Indeed, the purpose of our cultural tour is unique. Instead of exploring ancient ruins, our goal is to create them. Or, at least, that seems to be my goal this morning.

I feel so hostile! I'm somewhat disappointed in our first day in Seville. True, the old city is beautiful, especially walking through the narrow artistic streets of the Jewish section. If we were not staying in this flea-bag miserable hotel everything else would be fine. Even this hotel isn't so bad. It's just my expectations were so high and my room is so low.

Well, why complain? On the other hand, why not? That's what journal writing is for. Yesterday I was riding high on writing Sylvan Woods. Can't I do it again today? Every day is different. We'll see.

A Night of Tapas in Seville

How do I tell people about this one? Dance troupes galore. Flying Spanish feet. Stamping, singing, laughing, crying Sevillanas. Seeing a rehearsal of a top Seville dance troupe, and getting a private lesson in Sevillanas from the founder and director of Grupo de Danzas Ciudad De Sevilla, Joaquim Ruiz Postigo. Truth is, it is just too early to talk about it. But I would love to remember the Sevillanas he taught us.

There can be no denying the Mephistophelian aspects of nights beyond time.

I'm not in the mood to write anything this morning. Does that mean anything? Does my mood really matter? Or should I say, the hell with my mood, and just write anyway? Probably the latter. In fact, just saying it, facing the temporary deadness within, opening to the darkness of walls, towers, fixtures, and Jorge Canedas, can evidently open up a small passage inside the canals of my brain—the dwarf forms of Canedellias—and help pour for a wellspring of dancing mice. These grains beyond time can visissify the quandary of legends behind the wall.

This morning someone is looking over my shoulder. I'm writing with an audience in mind. Who is it? Natalie? Why? I don't know. She is in my writing class. Last night, Natalie, Mayta, and I walked back to the hotel together through the half lit streets of Seville. I spoke to Mayta "in private" in Natalie's presence. I said it's okay to talk because she is "in the family." Well, once I included her in the family who appeared in her place but my mother of course, who is now looking over my shoulder and judging my writing.

Goodbye black-crowed shoulder bird. Fly off my shoulder. Go back to the barn rafters where you belong.

Onwards and sidewards. The warm-up whir is happening. Faster and faster the fingers fly, faster and faster the mind races. That mind is mine!

Claustrophobia

Tight, gasping. It's claustrophobia. No time to myself. The walls of the tour have closed in. I'm incredibly tired—but this fatigue is more about claustrophobia than exhaustion. It happened in Bulgaria, too. I noticed it there, recognized it, dealt with it, and moved on.

Blessings

My claustrophobia is taking place even though I couldn't ask for a better group! Thus, it has nothing to do with the people on this tour. Rather, it has to do with the schedule and pacing. But more than that, it has to do with me. Awareness, self-awareness, is the only way to handle it. I've just done that. Claustrophobia has vanished. I'm back to loving this tour and the incredible experiences it is giving me. Can I handle them? Yes. After all, I did bring Fred Curtis's positive letter about my teaching of folk dancing at Drew University!

What an honor to organize, lead, and run such a tour! What an honor to be in Spain, have a wonderful guide like Mayte Jurado, and deal, in the distance, with Jorge Caneda, Alejandro Muniz, and Paco (Francisco), Mayte's father. When I can step out of myself, I realize I am blessed to lead and perform such work. After years of therapy, searching for my true self, for the loose, laughing, off-the-wall, mad shoe wild and wooly, running wild on the grass, pensive, thoughtful, artistic, dynamic, reclusive, in-room, out-in-public me, I finally have to say on days like this, I feel truly blessed to be put on this earth!

Duty

I'm starting off with a bunch of questions. Why? Probably because, as Elie Weisel said in *Night*, questions have a special power; they have more power than answers. I'm hoping that, by asking questions, I'll not necessarily come up with answers but rather, I'll jump start my mind which in turn will jump start my fingers, which will in turn jump start my writing. It must be working. I've already produced two paragraphs out of nothing. True, quality and meaning may suffer. But am I writing to create meaningful prose or to write every day no matter what. Indeed, I don't care if I produce pages of shit, volumes of junk. The main task is to write, write, write. Everything else will take care of itself.

So, now that I have jump-started my mind, what else is new? I'm reading about the Basques: Euskadi, and of San Sebastian, Bilbao, and even the capital of Navarre, Pamplona. I'm looking into Roncevalles, the "Song of Roland," and perhaps visiting Lourdes. I'm exploring the Pyrenees in search of new words. But mostly I'm exhausted. I'm stretching my mind in all directions, trying to rise above my mental and physical fatigue, reaching for an inspiration when I have none. All this is in the service of writing, for the purpose of fulfilling my quotas so I can walk the streets again today with head high.

Must I be inspired in order to write? In fact, must I be inspired to do anything? The obvious answer is: No. Witness these pages I have just produced. They were created with not a wit of inspiration, from a half-dead mind attached to a half-dead body nourished by a half-dead spirit. Any yet, they were produced.

What does all this mean? I can, must, should, and will go on in spite of inspiration. Call it a sense of duty.

Now there's a word I've never used before. Duty? Me, have a sense of duty? I never think of myself that way. I am free, a wild, unchained spirit roaming the Sierra Nevada mountains surrounding Granada, playing flamenco guitar under an olive tree in the groves of Jaén.

But indeed I do. My duty is to follow the writing trail. I am on the pilgrim's path, a lifetime trek to the miracle schedule, Santiago de Compostela, Galician land.

There is, evidently, no escape. I am not my own master, as I once thought. My duty is to "another." And this is true, even though that "other" is within me.

Voyage Straight to the Center

Maybe I'll buy a guitar in Granada today. Imagine that. First I'll play it. Then I'll sell it in America. Moving into the guitar selling business could be one of the excuses I need to return to Andalusia. A new business in the making.

But even more important psychologically is developing yesterday's idea of "going straight to the center." This would be a major jump for me.

By the way, yesterday I noticed as we were touring the Alhambra and walking through the gardens of Generalife (from the Arabic *genat-al-arif*—"genat" is garden, "arif" is architect (God): Garden of the Architect), my mind slipped or, I should say, soared straight out of the garden to the Canary Islands. I mentioned this to our guide, Mayta. She said you should stay in the present. First, I apologized by saying, yes, that is one of the lessons I have been put on earth to learn. Then I realized my answer was defensive. Why should I be defensive when my mind soars? Answer: I should not be. Only the old self from the old neighborhood would be defensive about such a thing. My defensive statement was not even true. Rather, I am in the present. I am certainly in the here-and-now when I am soaring! The gardens of Generalife in the Alhambra served as an inspiration! They lifted me out of my environment, put me on the a higher plane, and released my mind to soar into the higher realm of Canary Island imagination!

So ends our tour of Spain.

A Closet Choreographer Steps Out

Such adulation in Augusta, Georgia. I did a great job. Such respect and admiration. Wow!

I was treated like a master. I was the folk dance teacher's teacher. Bob said, "I learned it all from Jim. I started at just about zero, and learned how to folk dance at his feet." Over the years, Bob slowly become my right hand man, my best helper. He taught with me on folk dance weekends, lectured on exercise, grew and blossomed in the newly developing north Jersey folk dance world, much of which I started.

I am a master at this folk dance thing. If not me, who else? I've gone on all the trips. I was there, in Bulgaria, Hungary, Greece, Romania, Turkey, Israel, Tunisia, Russia, and more. I choreograph and lead with confidence because I know.

Nevertheless, I am not used to looking at myself as a master. It takes confidence to do it.

The new voice of this On My Own journal is one of growing confidence, security, stability, and mucho wahoos.

Bob also reminded me of many things I once said but I have since forgotten. Well, if not forgotten, at least they have sunk to the bottom of the pot. Seeing the group he has created, his attitude towards it, the fine dancers he has taught, was an affirmation of all the things I've done. Imagine that! My pupil out on his own and expanding the world. I started it, he expanded it. On the weekend, it felt like we both finished it.

Bob also reminded me that International folk dancing is a new art form. It is an American phenomenon. Although started in Germany, it developed in America. Look at the Teutonic word "volk, volk tanz," and its English form of "folk". But it needed America to expand. All other countries only dance their own ethnic dances. Americans, because we are the melting pot where so many cultures mix and blend, have created a venue where these dances can meet and blend together, and, in the process, create a new international folk dance form. In this form, we first remove the dances from their native culture, take out the social, party, food, drinking, family, live music, and celebration for a special-event (wedding, etc.) atmosphere, and keep only the dance itself.

The original folk dance is thus, somewhat naked when it arrives in America. We take this unclothed dance, place it in a rented room, play records, tapes, or CD's of it, and teach the steps to Americans who are not even part of these cultures. Thus is it totally new art form.

Why is this new form idea so important to know? Because it gives me "permission" to choreograph dances. Without it, I say to myself, how can I, an American, a foreigner, dare present a dance from "their" country and culture? I am not a native speaker. I did not grow up in the country. How can I say, the dance I created is from that country? And this, even though, after many years of travel and study, I know their dance styles very well.

The answer to this creative, artistic, and choreographic question is: in America, we are creating a new international folk dance form. I am free to create anything I like. Naturally, I try to learn as much as I can about these cultures, how they move, dance, think, eat, sleep, etc. But, no matter how much I know, I will never be them. I will only be me, an American who loves their dances. But, as an artist, creator, and lover, I can create new dances, and place them in the new American international folk dance repertoire.

I no longer have to be a closet choreographer. I can come out in the open. When teaching a dance, my own creation, I can even announce it to the group! Wow, imagine, admitting publically that I choreographed it! For this realization alone, I have to thank Bob and Chelley for their invitation to Georgia.

Folk Dance Clubs. . . or Making Money is so much Fun!

Folk Dance Clubs. The Jim Gold Folk Dance Club of Bedford: or the Bedford Folk Dance Club, led by Jim Gold. I don't know what title is best. But whatever I come up with, it could expand to all my folk dance classes. In concept, it is a totally new idea and a totally new beginning.

The registration fee will include membership. The Jim Gold Card. It entitles you to a certain number of classes, say ten, and/or a year's worth. Plus you get other benefits: $100–$200 off on a tour (depending what card you buy), $25 off on weekends, 10% to 20% off on boutique items (quarterly up-date mailings of "newsletter" etc?), a Jim Gold book. . . . Maybe that's it. Or maybe I'll think of something else.

The registration card would cost around $125 ($150? less?) for ten weeks, or a semester. (Or maybe $135 or $145 for twelve weeks). One could also take all and any class during that ten–twelve week period. I would also offer a one-year membership at say $500 ($495), which might include $200 off for tours and all classes!

My idea would be to try to get everyone in all my folk dance classes to register.

Naturally, I won't succeed in getting everyone to register. For those who do not, the one-time people, the visitors and occasional drop-ins, I would charge $15 at the door. This fee would be credited toward their registration.

The beauty of all this is obvious. If it works, there is the possibility that I could actually make a living teaching folk dancing! If it doesn't work, then I can spend my newly created "free time" promoting and selling things that do make money such as my tours, club dates, and concert bookings. Folk dance teaching would become a side-line, a "hobby."

But why even bother thinking this way. Truth is, part of me does not see how this can possibly not work! It is such a good idea. It is a wonderful motivating idea! First of all, it would motivate me to actually go out and sell folk dancing! It would be worth putting in the effort. It would be worth spending time writing press releases, placing ads in the paper, even calling potential folk dancers and asking them to register! This because I would be selling registrations, which cost actual money, namely ten-twelve weekers at $125-$145, or annual memberships at $495. I would be putting my efforts into building something worthwhile, worthy, and worth money. I would be supporting my survival. Best of all, I would not resent my efforts but rather, love them, be enthusiastic about them, find even some joy and ecstasy in them. And this because making money, real money, is so much fun!

Egypt

I met Milton Wheeler, from William Carry College in Hattiesburg, Mississippi, on our flight from Cairo to Aswan. An inspirational character and tour leader. He books his hotels directly, saves money, and protects himself through a bonding company.

Would I want to try booking hotels, and even bus and driver directly? The challenge here is getting lower rates and saving money. But it's more headaches, too. I it worth a try?

Climbing Mount Sinai

Fear for my life!

Death, awe, chilling fear, darkness, dread, cold and discomfort were my main feelings climbing Mount Sinai, Gebel Musa, Mount Horeb.

Were these the feelings Moses felt?

Fear and awe may come before wonder. Wonder appeared in the

awesome beauty of this dry desert mountain. But I was mostly too tired, and frightened, to appreciate it. Visiting St. Catherine's Monastery at the foot of Mount Sinai, and seeing the original burning bush and well of Jethro was pleasant in its safety.

Climbing Mount Sinai means revisiting the role of fright, fear, and awe in my life.

It is, after all, such a dominant factor even though we humans, in the safeties of our modern civilization, so often try to deny it.

Fear often precedes beauty; awe precedes wonder.

Summarizing my thoughts the day after climbing Mount Sinai: A thrilling, chilling experience with mystical ramifications so deep it will take me a long time to fathom them.

Meditate on the awesome energy of fear and its connection to God Himself.

On Reaching the Summit

The summit of Mount Sinai is where, according to tradition, God appeared in the form of a cloud of fire. He spoke to Moses.

What did I do when I reached the summit? I sat down on a rock and fell asleep. I hardly looked at dawn's rising sun. I just hoped the whole climbing experience would end and I could go home, sleep in my safe warm bed, and maybe go out for Chinese food.

More on the Mount Sinai Summit

Sinatic changes: Calm is rocking my foundation. Inner peace screams across the desert. the wadis (valleys), filled with shifting sands, cry in their beer.

Fun and freedom loom deep on the horizon.

I walk through the streets of Cairo with a new post-Sinai freedom and fun.

Climbing up Mount Sinai, slowly over the days, months, and years. I pass through the gates. I reach the majestic, wind-strewn summit of fun and freedom!

What does climbing Mount Sinai represent? The inner climb

over rock passes of fear, high steps over terror, past gates of panic, awe, and death. At last one reaches the dawn, sun-drenched summit of Cairo-walking fun and freedom!

I am in a joyous release.

Sadness vanishes through the Nile gates of the sixth cataract. Joy and fun of freedom rush in to take its place.

An amazing transformation.

Dollars Sailing Down The Danube!

After a day of walking through Budapest, I returned to our Artotel on foot. As I crossed the Lanchid Bridge on my way from Pest to Buda, I saw a beggar on the bridge. Yesterday when I crossed, I had seen him on the other side of the bridge. Today, when I passed him, I put some money in his hand. He thanked me.

Why am I giving to beggars?

It all started when I understood my true attitude towards money: If I like to run wild with it, and money is simply a fun instrument, then why not give in to its charm and play with it?

How?

One way is: Give it to beggars.

How can that be fun?

Well, first of all, beggars are very appreciative. They smile and say thank you. Sometimes they say it enthusiastically. Or, if they are sad beggars and doing their sad bit, they thank you mournfully. But no matter how you look at it, by giving them a quarter or even a dollar—small amount by today's entertainment standards—you are getting a heartfelt thank you. Sometimes it is even accompanied by a smile and thankful eye contact.

But, you protest, it's fake. Beggars are putting on an act. Well, I say, how often do you get an act for only a quarter or dollar? Look at the price of Broadway and off-Broadway shows.

Plus you have the added benefit of actual human contact.

Compare this kind of giving to sending your favorite charity a check. First of all, you never even know where your money is going. Administration, secretaries, and salaries eat up most of your money. Who knows how much of it actually goes to the needy. Second, you never see a smile or hear a thank you (although you might get a written form-letter thank you in the mail). There is no human face attached to your giving. You are throwing your money into the wind. But when you hand it to beggars, they stands directly in front of you; you are face to face with an actual human being! And you can see the effect of your giving in shining thankful eyes.

How many times do you hear thank you in a day, anyway? How many times a day is your existence appreciated? How often are you thanked for being here on earth?

What about the beggar's benefits, you ask. Shouldn't the money you give improve his situation, help them better their social position, feed or cloth them, perhaps even help them get an education? Will the beggar knows how to "spend it correctly?" Will he or she use it for drugs? After considering all these possibilities you usually end up giving nothing. Why waste your hard earned money, you say.

But I say you should give the beggar your money because it's fun! Period. That's it. Fun is its own reward. If the beggar decides to throw the money in the river, well, it's also fun to see dollars sailing down the Danube.

Most of our tour group went to the flea market. But some chose to attend the Transylvanian folk dance workshop in the Fono cultural house. I did the latter and ended up having lunch with Flo and Joe. We spoke about many things and I ended up telling them about my tours. I told them I had raised my prices several years ago, I told them why. I said I was proud of my prices.

I am proud of my prices because I am proud of my tours. They are quality services and quality adventures. Their price, in a more subtle way, tells this.

I left the table however, feeling proud and happy. My feet and mind were smiling.

Our tour was coming to an end. I had done a fine job. Competent, well-rounded, well-pasted together. It's time to pack, think about the next leg of this journey, and to sing praises and hallelujahs. I have nothing specific to be happy about; only a general feeling of inner radiance, and contentment. Perhaps this is enlightenment in its Budapest form. Or at least its Buddha- Pest incarnation.

The Vilmos Szabadi Connections

Our tour feels easy. With ease comes inner peace.
Notice the word "our" instead of "my."
Where does "our" fit into "my?"
After the concert at the Bartok House last night I went backstage to meet the solo violinist Vilmos Szabadi.
"Wonderful concert," I said. "You're an excellent violinist and performer. Have you ever toured the United States?"
"I'm coming there in three months," he answered.
"Who is your agent?"
"A Hungarian man. His name is Kalman Magyar."
"Does he live in Teaneck?" I asked.
Vilmos looked surprised. "Yes. How did you know?"
"On Oakdene Avenue?"
"Yes."
"He's fifteen blocks from my house. He was my first Hungarian dance teacher, and helped me organize my first tour to Hungary in 1984!"
We both laughed in amazement at this "coincidence!" But notice the exclamation point.
"Do you know the violinist Attila Falvay?" I asked.
"Of course. He is lots of fun."
"His father, Charles Falvay, was the folk dance teacher and folklore guide on our first Hungarian tour. I've know him for years, too."
How these lines of communication moved! I thought, since I'm in Budapest I should call Charles and say hello. Then I thought, I should call Kalman, say hello, then have lunch with him, renew old contacts. I haven't really talked to him in years. Charles, too.
I thought about former friends and colleagues I haven't seen or spoken to in years, and the question emerged: Where do others fit into my life? How important are they? Is it "worth the effort" to try fitting them into my life? How important are people to me in general? What, if anything, do they have to do with my inner world, the world of my imagination where the real me lives?
On one level, it is a shame to lose contact with these fine people.

I had wonderful times with them. Is there another level?

Audrey said the "coincidental meetings" I am having with Vilmos Szabadi and his agent relationship with Kalman Magyar, and with Charles Falvay at the Fono House is a validations of my good works. That would be nice.

Could it be true?

Jewish Macho

I wonder if my attraction to suffering, my temptation to give in and even wallow in pain, has something to do with being Jewish. Does the Jewish part me feel guilty if it doesn't suffer?

Suffering is even a kind of Jewish macho. The strength to bear it, the ability to stand it. Somehow suffering improves and upgrades you.

"Oy vey, vat pain! But I'm Jewish; I can take it. I vouldn't gif it up for de vorld."

Jews have the tikkun olam commandment to heal the world. I can't be happy until everyone else is. Thus I'm in pain until everyone else is happy.

Jews have to cure the world first. Only after everyone is happy and cured can they stop suffering.

Is my attraction to suffering and the pain stimulant a cultural thing?

Business As A Miracle!

Miraculous things keep happening in my business. But it is so fraught with disappointments, fears, worries, and annoyances that I am often unable to see its miraculous qualities.

For a moment at the airport I melted down with the "Thank God, it's over!" feeling. Even though I wore the cloak of responsibility easily on this tour, it was, nevertheless, a weight.

No more. The tour is over.

But my weight was light, my cry, a blip. I'm feeling quiet satisfaction.

On the plane back to New York, Flo showed me her Allende

book. I opened it. The first page said: "A wise man is always joyful."

I called Eileen Rogers to ask her about going on tour to Morocco with us.

She said, "On my calendar I have more doctor's appointments than social appointments."

I said "Why not consider doctor's appointment as social appointments, and social appointments as doctor's appointments?"

She liked it. So did I.

Why not consider my sales calls as social appointments? Sales calls as way of socializing. After all, I like the people I call. Selling them something gives me the "excuse" to call them. A leisurely conversation with the sales aspect "dropped on the side" makes my call so much more pleasant.

"More pleasant" is the way to go.

Business as Part of My Miracle Schedule

There is a gutsy excitement to business. Knowing this enables me to add business to my miracle schedule.

Nevertheless, I tremble at the thought. Until now, "business" has had so much repression in it. Can such a former monster actually enter the sacred inner realm of miracle schedule? Will I allow this dragon into my castle? Can such a creature join my beautiful world of guitar, writing, yoga, running, and study? Evidently, hard-edged and practical business can coalesce with dreams created and emboldened in the artistic, mystical chamber of my Imagination.

Folk Dance Sales Campaign

Promoting folk dancing as my base will increase attendance at weekends and tours. It has to be promoted as a good-in-itself. I also need more attendees for my emotional well being.

This year's goal: Increase folk dance class attendance.

This means a publicity, public relations, advertising, and promotional campaign. It even means calling people to encourage them to attend.

Raise my prices: Charge $15 ($12?) at the door, but $10 per class for "members," that is, those who have registered for a series of classes.

Rivers Are Rolling Again

Rivers are rolling: Business has become part of my miracle schedule.

I see how important the tour business is for me. It is a personal and motivating factor both financially and in my studies. It represents two vital pillars of my miracles schedule: Studies, and finance (business).

My God, what am I saying? Business as part of my miracle schedule? In the past, there was nothing about business that made it part of my miracle schedule. No miracles in it. Too concrete, of-this-world, material, and worldly. But when success in it comes through registrations and checks in the mail it always makes me feel great. Warmth, love, and happiness floods my being.

My happiness dependent on others? In the past, I could not accept this. Too emotionally risky. Fraught with danger and old-time hurts.

But somehow the walls between the business world and my "true self" have fallen away. I am open. . . and free to recognize my dependence others. It has freed me to include business in my miracle schedule. It has also collapsed the wall between the artistic room of my imagination and the formerly cold, heartless, crack-down, mean, miserable outside world. The outside world now has both love and misery, fear and fire, dependence and independence. Moreover, I can now be part of it, see it within myself, join the armies crossing the plains, the wild jeeps and roaring airplanes crossing the Afghan deserts, attacking the caves of my mind, freeing its prisoners to enter the world as free men.

Rivers are rolling again.

Sales as the Missing Link to Motivation

The ice is breaking, breaking, breaking.

I am forming a new relationship to others based on sales. Selling pushes me to call, contact, and stay in touch with others. Without sales motivation, friends remain friends but truth is, I hardly ever call them. This even includes my family and closest friends. They stay in the background as a support system. But since they are not customers, not connected to money, sales, and business survival, they are, sadly, not as "vitally important" to me in the present.

Evidently, selling gives a vital meaning to my life.

This is a shocking, stunning, upsetting, and, down the road, inspirational realization. It is a totally new understanding of sales and its relationship to me.

The vital juices in sales which I have, up to now, denied may well be the missing link in daily motivation.

Calling My Former Folk Dancers!

Practical sales application:

I can start by calling former folk dancers! Invite them back to dancing. I am not looking for new dancers, but old ones with experience, who are not starting from scratch. Of course, if new ones come they will be welcome, integrated into the group, and taught accordingly. But I am now trying to build up a fun dance evening for myself.

Sales call up my fighting energy. They make me feel alive.

Sales energize me. That is their miracle!

Sales Mind Fitting into My Body

Maybe that is why my body aches so much. I'm in transition. Growing pains. My body is growing in order to fit in my new sales mind.

Evidently, I always had a "secret love" of sales. Only it was expressed through hatred.

Hate can turn into love. Passionate hatred can, under the right circumstances, turn into passionate love.

The foundation of both is passion.

God

Sometimes the answer to prayers is "Yes."
Sometimes it is "No."
Sometimes it is "Wait."

The Prison Of Certainty

A focus on playing without mistakes is to focus on certainty. A focus on certainty is a focus on limitations.

Certainly can be its own prison.

Certainty is limitation. It frees you from fear. . . but also boxes you in.

Ego demands specifics. God offers the Infinite.

Asking to play guitar with no mistakes or with incredible technical prowess is asking for little. But playing with an attitude of "Thy Will Be Done," I play in a field of infinity.

Embracing uncertainty, riding its whirlpool path of infinite possibility, can bring you strength, strenght, power, and freedom.

Terror is connection to the infinite.
But we are usually too terrified to realize it.

Do not lose your sense of wonder among the intellectual weeds.
Read slowly. . . and with astonishment.

On Communicating The Ineffable

Awe and wonder do not exist in solid form. As the Great Invisible and Great Intangible, they are ineffable.

Then I went for a run. As I turned the corner in Bergenfield during my second hour I had a revelation: Awe and wonder can be communicated. But only indirectly through the subtle vibrations.

People often sense something good is happening but can't explain why. "I loved your concert! Why? I don't know. I can't explain it. I just loved it!"

Personally, this means I can communicate awe and wonder. When I teach dance, play guitar, or sit still, my vibrations are sent out to others. As they send out positive vibrating messages, the deepest inner part in others knows...and smiles.

Abraham Joshua Heschel says, "God is holy, different, and apart from all that exists. I say, God is holy, different, and within all that exists. Intellectually, these are opposites. But spiritually, is there really a difference? Aren't we simply "playing with words?" And just because "apart" and "within" appear to be totally different, on a higher plane, couldn't they be the same?
I think so.

Awe and wonder is Judaism at its best.

Charisma is the ability to radiate your God connection.

Judaism is about remembering the God connection.

God and Abandonment

God expelled Adam and Eve out of the Garden of Eden because they broke the rules.
Does God reject rule breakers? Does He abandon them?
Or, is it we who abandon Him?
God has given man has free choice. It appears He expelled Adam and Even from the Garden of Eden because they broke His rules. But suppose Adam and Eve simply refused to take responsibility for their decision. What if they were afraid to face the terrors of their own freedom. Suppose, instead of accepting responsibility, they decided to blame their actions on God.
"He did it! He threw us out! We're innocent victims. Sure, we decided to eat an apple. Big deal. Why make such a fuss? Just because He said don't do it? Who's He, anyway? We'll do what we want! No one can push us around! If we want to eat apples, we'll eat apples. If we want to talk to serpents, we'll talk to serpents! We're in charge of our lives. We're free to decide. Whatever happens happens. Damn the consequences!"
Now that would be Adam and Eve taking responsibility.

However, as biblical cowards, they decided to blame their decisions and actions on God.

Does God abandon man?

It is impossible. Not only is God omnipotent, he is also omnipresent. He is everywhere, in everything and everyone. How can He disappear? How can He reject anyone or anything when He is their very essence? He would be, in effect, rejecting Himself. True, God, being omnipotent, has the power even to reject Himself. But why would He do such a thing?

God's rejection and abandonment of man is thus an impossibility. Only man can reject God. And he sometimes does, often with a vengeance. That is his choice. It's part of free choice and the learning process.

Breaking illusions is a step on the path to Oneness.

On Mosaic Law

Why do I resist Mosaic Law?

Someone outside is telling me what to do, demanding I perform in a certain way. I have not been consulted or even considered.

Mosaic Law seems to come from outside.

But suppose it was born within? Suppose these God-given Laws existed and were then discovered by individuals instead of a so-called outside force that Moses named God.

If God is within, why shouldn't these Laws be within, too?

Thus, why shouldn't these Laws be my Laws?

I can speak to Him directly. He may tell me I need Mosaic Laws. But then I will "own" them. They will be my Laws, too.

Since all is within, why not assume the Mosaic Laws, and the Torah are within, too. They are part of my vision.

According to Judaism, man is made in God's image.

Killing a man is an offense against God.

But the very notion that God can be offended is absurd.

Such "personalizing" of God may contribute to enforce ethics. Not a bad thing. The ethics are good. But, as far as using God to enforce them, absurd.

The Ten Commandments are Moses' invention. He credited

them to God. He was right. All creation comes from God, including the Aserot Hadibrot. But they were filtered through the mind of Moses. Moses and God get the credit. They were a team.

Everyone is on that team.

Everyone in this world is on the same team.

Inventions

Let Cheesecake Fly!

What of Heraclitus? Was this ancient Greek philosopher really Hairy Clitorus? Did he change his name to avoid taxes?

When will these drivels of dried meat be lifted from my back? Why hoist so many ships? Can't I live like a bird and fly like one, two? Break the fetid fetters, leap the grave, embrace limestone, and run down the street singing paeans, draping our loins with burgundy scarves, and waving banners from Bloomingdales. I'm tired of runt existence. Unfurl the flags! Let cheesecake fly!

Sinking is part of rising. Soon I'll return to Norway surrounded by seas of sucking whirlpools and monster trolls where the only parasite is an old Norse dictionary and the only cartoon is Looney Runes.

Whooping dunderwarts! Dingle my dinnersleeves! It is sun rise time. Wet nutrients, filled with soup suds of a pristine yogic nature fly through the bent steel kitchen. Purple curtains smacked with marmalade stand but once on their hind legs.

When was once? Of course it was during the domination of medieval Bulgarian capital, Veliko Turnovo. That "once" is related to "one ce," where "ce" connotes the "cent" of one hundred per cent which later translated into the Bulgarian rose perfume industry centered at Kazanluk and became one hundred per "scent." Many a nail barrel rolled down the Balkan mountains on this once.

And yet, a bellowing sad caterwaul from the mountain top. There, dressed in March rags, stands the medieval Bulgarian architects dream, Castle-Upon-Soup-Pristine. Henry Lucenwarts of Tulip, venerable pisswater and pusswetter Hercules dental family, dongs his dinner bell. Here comes Valley Maiden, sweet apron in hand, yogocic blunderbuss on foot. "Shall I cough up a soup for you this morning, sire?" she asks. Gently, she kneels before Lord Turnip of Tulip, cleans a dong with her purple foot, then rests her wine cellar of animal basements on his knee. "How I long before your turnip, sire?" she sighs.

"My garden is growing daily," quoths Tulip. "Surely, a piglet from your Warp-and-Whyre will come along soon. Then you can cake and eat tit."

"I prefer having your rake and beat it," quoths the sweet Val Hen.

"Chickens have always been my favorite food."

"My favorite foot as well," says sire Tulip. "I prefer a roast foot over the boiled."

"Is your brain tired this morning, sire? Can you not hear the soft-click difference between "d" and "t?""

"Fatigue is exactly what is troubling me. How did you know, my sweet Prince Pea?"

"Princess Pea, please! Sire, why do you ad the masculine touch to my feminine endings?"

"I like it because I like it, sweet Valley. But could your secret identity be sweet Fal of Fal-acy ? Are you a fallacy in feminine clothing? Do you really exist?"

"Ah, such existence questions are not for my feminine ears this morning. Let us continue tonight when I return half-baked."

Hell Travel

Once there was a tooth fairy named Root Canal. Her friends called her Ruth.

Ruth came from the Hebrew-Anglo-Saxon etymological root "pity" or "compassion." But Ruth had no pity or compassion. She loved drilling holes in teeth. Her greatest pleasure came drilling beneath a tooth, straight into gums and nerves! How she loved hearing her victims scream! She loved driving their mouths crazy. Holding throbbing gums, they ran down the street waving their arms, and screaming for all the sewers to hear. "Help, help! Attack of the Root Fairy! Save us! We'll give you a free trip to the dentist!"

Thus did Root Fairy's "clients" run around town.

Ruth loved it. "I want to give them even more pain!" she purred. "I'm a giving person. Pain is what I give best. How will people know what pleasure is if they have no pain? I deliver the dark side with vengeance and love. I think I'm doing God's work although I must say He does not recognize our Amalgamated Pain Professionals Union of America. We tried joining the AFL last year, but their president told us to go to Hell. I went there for a visit. Lots of "Pain Professionals" like myself down there, people who glory in giving good service.

People sometimes ask: Am I guilty about my work?

"I once was. After recognizing certain faults and mental deficiencies I went to see another pain professional, Larry the Psychotherapist. He gave me plenty of pain, most of it mental. I understand this kind, because I give it to others, too. Root canal is physical and mental. That's why I tried joining Larry's union, United Couches of America. But they rejected us, too.

In those early days of my career, it hurt to realize my job was to create pain. But it hurt more when no clients came. During the first few months of my practice I had to give pain away. Nobody would buy it. I was on welfare for years. But when the government cut back funding for the Pain Professionals Support Services Division, I knew I'd soon be out on the street. Imagine, a homeless pain professional! How would I do my root canal work without an office?

For a year, I worked for nothing. I was reduced to performing dental work on broccoli stalks! How depressing. Those were really down times.

Finally, I got so frustrated I decided to fry myself. It didn't work. Then I tried boiling. Nothing. I tried other methods of suicide. None worked. That was when I realized I was immortal. After that I didn't mind being kicked around and vilified by the press. Rejections by the unions didn't bother me either. After all, they are merely temporal. In a hundred years or so, the press and all my critics will be gone. But I'll be around forever. That's something to be proud of. What other business person can say that?

Speaking of business, I started a new one. My visit to Hell really inspired me. I ended up creating a whole new way of travel! And all because when someone told me to go to Hell, I went! After many visits, I decided to run tours there. I started my own travel company. I called it Hell Travel. The Pain Professionals Union really loves it. Several of my friends are now working with me, too.

I'm amazed at the response we're getting. If others tell you to "Go to Hell!" our tour company can accommodate you. There's a huge market for this kind of travel. Our add in the New York Times simply reads: "Go to Hell. . . with us!"

Economy tours start at $995. With this basic itinerary you get your fires but with only one pitch fork stabbing performed by a character from a Hieronymous Bosch painting.

How do we decide on prices?

Hell has many levels or "circles." Prices depend on how many you visit. For example, Economy Hell tours give you one circle. Although not as in-depth as the pricier tours, you nevertheless get a general picture of life below. You meet the people, dance with the natives, and acquire an overall view of what might be your future.

We don't limit our tours to the living. We promote among the dead as well. But, of course, we charge them a lower rate.

Luxury Hell tours start at $4,995. On these tours you visit every level. Dante only wrote about nine circles. But he never really went to Hell himself except in his imagination. He added Purgatory and Paradise both to attract more readers and soften the blow. We soften nothing. Our tours are just plain hell. Plus, we offer more circles than Dante. Twenty-six, to be exact. We've also added root canal and psychotherapy at no extra cost.

Thus I have turned rejection into a flourishing business. You can do it, too. But if you are rejected, please don't go to Hell. I don't want any competition.

The Larry Henry Story

Isn't this the time for the appearance of Larry Henry, famous biblical schizophrenic? They are also known as Larry and Henry, the only schizophrenic (s) to climb Mount Sinai with Moses. Larry—or was it Henry—tried to stamp out the burning bush. Biblical writers eradicated him. Not a mention of this split mind anywhere, no Greek iota of print, not even a comma in the Septuagint, Pentateuch, Hamesh Hamisha, or anything else. They burnt his blood in calves' milk, then drowned him with his golden calf in the waters of the Nile. Hard to get portage on that one. Finally, Aaron carried off Henry—or was it Larry?

Lithuanian Pooperpill

Sounding the clowns! Bring them on, dancing, laughing, and prancing down the airpit runway of Laternine Airlines. Yes, we're flying off to Lithuania with nary a parry in stock. Each one of our customers is wearing a full-suit of goose wings. Indeed, we are flying the air bus of our choice. Blue-green hemispheres straddle each seat. Window seat, indeed. But who wants an aisle? And who needs one when windows march down the aisle just as the aisles march out the windows? It is a strange plane, indeed. But what do I know about Lithuanians, anyway? Almost nothing. Strange. I am traveling to the land of Baltic madness with not a brain thought in sight. My head is totally empty for this one. Where in my Estonian landing, Latvian sandwich, St. Petersburg caviar, or my Lithuanian pooperpill?

Nowhere in sight, that's where. Strange. Indeed, it is strange. Strange, indeed. Indeed, strange. Indeed, and out of deed, too.

Nothingness and emptiness are the highest purposes of this tour into the dark northern snowlands hidden south and beneath the subterranean mountains of Lapland where reindeer dwell in perpetuity, and hidden suns, somnambulant and whirling, mount the helpless stars from behind. Talk about creations of new universe?

Avalanches Are Silenced

Clouds of pooperpill sail across the living room table causing the air to be thick with rain and sand. Young, Wader Gilpoopenheim, first herculean ancestor of the Mars and Venus faction, sits in his oven drinking beer. Far to the north, in the town of Hammerklavier-Upon-Key, a tinker bell rings. There, in her cardboard home, sits the worthy Florence Peepingtom reading pages of the cobbler's kabbalah. Her pink and woven body, fashioned of Palatine marble, grey paint, and fences, waddles towards fulfillment on the Hudson river bank.

"Finally, the turds have come home to roost," she says, sanding her playpen with a turbine blaster. Boards of fresh-plied hooey guard her baby brain and protect each milk faucet from the greedy sniping hands of the Superfluous Pharoahs Outreach Program.

"This is not a time to gloat, mother," pipes Donald Walrus-Duck, worthy nephew of Queen Tut and Titti. His circumcised tusk rises in rebellion before swatting the Nile River fly squadrons sailing by on their way to visiting a closed coffin in Byzantium. His pants in an uproar, Donald cries,"I'll not be stopped!.

"Ottomans cannot be hatched before morning quills arrive."

Post-luncheon chatter quickly turns his dillies into a peepeeworth. Quickly Wide Mother Tut sits on him, squashes his adenoids, squeezes his adrenaloids, quells the storm in his liver, and squelches his thyroid, and extinguishes his barbecue

The rebel turnip turns silent.

An asteroid floats by with a throaty hiss.

Avalanches are silenced as a star slides into the mud.

Strip Mower Larry

Larry was a strip mower. He carved words on the strips while he sang. That's how he kept the elephants away. These flying jumbos attacked daily, dropping plum bombs of stewed molasses on his nest-worm head, clogging infant molecules of thought even as he breast-fed on tasty inner morsels of leaking brain bits.

Larry loved to suck luscious bulbous tits. But he couldn't admit it. Oh, no, not him! "I bite nails! I eat bullets!" he'd boast to his macho friends as they sat around the pool hall drinking beer, squashing roaches with their fingers, or stamping on rats scurrying across the floor. Wearing his clob-nobbed, hob-nailed. bob-hobbed combat boots, he often stooped to lick the animal blood off his heel, a contortionist feat he developed in the Taiwanese army during the Termite War of Rebellion of 1846. He also believed his ears served as antenna by the secret service to spy on Ancient Maggie, his mother-in-law of former years.

The mirrored window's of Maggie's house on the hill looked inward so she could see herself at every turn and bend. She loved to peer into toilets daily and predict the future through their flush. The seat cover had a picture of Plato.

Larry himself had grown up in a sanitation-oriented family. Strongly oriented towards orthodoxy, he worshiped at the altar of Higher Seated Ovals while attending classes at the University of Urological Navigation. That's why he fainted on Fine False Day when the landlord came to visit.

It is Stew Day and Jucent Peabody is happiest turnip farmer in the field. His garden has been planted with wines from Picardy. Bottles of ancient booze from Batavians up north, along with a few Frisian swigs have just sauntered in. Two hours ago the closes on their locks diked.

Indeed, a land locked holler can't be found among any bicycles here. Three times a day of Peabody writes. It is a good idea. It oils the joints and keeps pedals from slipping.

A squiggly bottom of a bygone booby snatchers walked headway into the herring refrigerator, boxing up bean carts, and turning orange juice containers into rubber necking traffic jams. Such vine fruit refrigerants could not be tolerated by Larry Refrigerator of Amsterdam's Wiry Suburb where fruit flies grow. Bumping sidewards through the canals, working backward in a whirl and whorl of insect chatter mixed with mosquito netting, he swatted the Great Ones, those doop swooping downers from Batavian whose Frisian canals dumped stingers in foul, fetid, and foolish waters. Denizen turisticas Amsterdamus: a new homo Hollandaise with sapient flesh now invading the north-baked shores of Stir Dam of Am.

Zane's Brain

What's in Zane's brain?

Yesterday I had a chance to examine it with my magnificence microscope. Here's what I saw:

A giant fire burns on the right side of Zane's Brain. It must be hundreds, thousands, even perhaps a million miles high. It shoots flame into the sky, burns planets, the Milky Way, and several galaxies.

On the left side of Zane's Brain is a great lake. It must be hundreds, thousands, even perhaps a million miles wide. It is very peaceful and beautiful. It sits there quietly absorbing the sun.

One day, the Fire in Zane's brain had an idea. "I'm dynamic, creative, innovative, adventurous, curious, expansive, and smart," it said. "I like to experiment and try out new things. Today I'll try something different. I'm going to make some money." Fire scratched its hot head thoughtfully. "Should I steal or borrow it? Well, borrowing is just plain boring. I'm going to steal it! That's exciting and fun. I'll steal a dollar and I'll some pizza with it. Then I'll steal $10, then $20,

$100, $1,000...one million dollars! I'll soon be the richest fire in the world! I'll steal more and more until I steal the whole world. What will I do with the world once I steal it? I'll burn it, of course. "Ha, ha, ha! That's what fires do!"

Fire laughed diabolically for fourteen days. Then it stopped. "Wait a minute, "it thought. "I'm part of the world. If I burn up the world, I'll destroy myself! That's not a good idea. I don't want to die! Maybe this isn't a good idea after all."

And Fire sat down on a hot stump to think it over.

Meanwhile Lake heard how Fire wanted to steal and then destroy the world. "That hothead!" said Lake. "I'm part of the world, too. I don't want to die. Fire gets carried away with himself sometimes. He doesn't know what to do with his extra energy. I'd better stop him before it's too late."

Beneath his calm surface, Lake made waves. "I'm going to dump my water on his stupid fire-filled head! I'm going to dampen him. He won't destroy me!"

Lake dumped 50 million buckets of water on Fire. SSSSSS, Fire's desire to steal a million dollars fizzed down to $1000, $100, $20, $10, $1, and finally to zero. His flames relaxed.

"Thanks, Lake," he said. "I'm feel much better. I don't know what came over me. I just got too hot, I suppose."

Then Fire took Lake by the hand, and they went out for pizza.

Wow, Look At That!

Once there was a little girl who said,

"Wow, look at that!" When she saw the sidewalk she'd shout: "Wow, look at that!" When she saw a car or airplane, she'd say: "Wow, look at that!" When she saw a bird, mouse, dog, cat, flower, tree, pony, man, woman, or child, she'd shout: "Wow, look at that!"

One day a bad fairy came to her house and said. "You're a stupid moron! Don't you know it is impolite to shout: 'Wow, look at that!?' It is wrong. Things are not the way they seem. Dogs rot, cats die, chickens get roasted, flowers fade, children age, men and women die and leave you, cars break down, planes get rusty, mice get run over by cars and rot on the street. The world is full of misery. Remember that next time you want to say 'Wow, look at that!'

The girl felt terrible. How could she have been so wrong? Soon she said nothing when she left the house. Her smile faded. Her eyes grew dead. Her face flattened.

She got sadder. But she couldn't even cry because now she thought that smart little girls didn't do that. One day she lay down on her living room floor and fell asleep. A distant dream reminded her that once upon a time the world had been filled with awe and wonder.

Then another fairy appeared. "Hello," it said. "I'm the good fairy. Bad fairy and I work together, teaching little girls. We're really the same fairy, but we wear disguises. Bad fairy teaches you to feel sad, and hit bottom. Why? So when you wake :up and see the bottom you know the best thing is: Point to it and say: 'Wow, look at that!'

The Wind And The King

Once a Wind came to visit a castle.

The King walked out to meet the Wind.

He loved her.

"Let us get married," he said.

The Wind answered, "Join me first. Let us play in the wild universe together."

"Ah, I would love that," said the King. "But I live in a castle. What will happen to my subjects? They cannot live without a king. I cannot live without them.

"Let us build a new castle for my kingdom and us."

The Wind thought about loss of freedom and responsibility as she pondered the question.

"Expect Nothing. Get Everything"

In Turnbull's biography, *Life Among The Cows*, Angus Bovine Huxley explains: "Turnbull's uncanny ability to fertilize vast arenas of nothingness, plant seeds in the Void, and fill volumes of space with even more space, has made him on of the top fertilizer and stock market analysts. In the process, he has become a rich man. His motto:

"Turn nothing into more nothing," has caught on throughout the financial world and all its global markets. Young people on planets, asteroids, and galaxies are forming John Turnbull Investment Clubs. One such club, the "Club V", located in Haircunt County on the asteroid Venus-Upon-Venal, is making quite a financial killing by selling space in vacant entrances. They plan to expand operations to large intestines and have opened up a new branch to investigate futures in the esophagus market.

Turnbull has other plans as well. With full Turnbull confidence, he says, "If I can turn nothing into more nothing I believe that, as my skills develop, I will one day be able to turn something into something else. Eventually, with enough capital, time, and investment savvy, I'll turn nothing into something! Thus, a zero investment would yield vast sums. Asking nothing of others yields an incredible return. This is investment at its best!"

The Turnbull philosophy, "Expect nothing. Get everything." is presently plastered on every John Turnbull Investment Club door.

The second century Greek philosopher, Diogenes Egocentric asked: "What is the most difficult thing in the world?"

He sid kick Valocentric answered: "Be your true self."

Then he asked: "What is even more difficult than that?"

Valocentric answered: "Be your true self in front of others."

Whacking the Tulip

Dandelion Jim sucked on his deep sadness down in the Dump Bar. His dirty finger nails, covered with matzah ball grease and stinkstew of melon purple, dug deep into the mud-plugged bottom of Tertiardary Land. His tomahawk, a pubic entry to public lives and prior rhythms, could not fathom the pitifully gaunt space of wiry primogeniture, primodenture, and primo dental service so far below.

He shouted from his perch on the tulip stand: "Will all wigwams present please stand up!"

But no Indian present could buy a tepee worth a damn.

Well, that's the way it is when Primo the Genital stands pat. He wakes often for morning service. But today he will not rise up for the occasion. He is furtive and clinging this morning. Will Dander Hip, his running mate, ever cease to bring in the blossoms?

This was the question asked by detective Hairy Lip Hip, gastronomic and whitewashed intestinal directory for the Isles of Langerhorn hockey team. "Puck, puck," he said. "Can a pancreas really skip past a lymph gland? Will a liver ever scream into the incendiary soup? And what of Jack the Ripper Duodenum? Will his pajamas crease before the spermatic onslaught of Muenster cheese gone wild in the deli?"

Wild, wild. Mrs. Sadness sat in the stew washing potatoes for the afternoon army lunch. "Hello, Mrs. Sadness. Won't you please come in? Would you like a chair for Squashed Potato, your evening accompanist?"

"Indeed, I would." Mrs. Sadness gnashed her teeth. A lean, mean look crossed her rutted face. She readied her hand to grab a pound of flesh from hench person, Jack the Unripper. His tulip had unfolded early that morning.

Mrs. Sadness's evil eyes swung left and right. They whacked the dandelion under Central Eyeball Station just before the train came in. "Ho, Ho, Cuss, eh?" she snarled. "Will you ever staunch the mad dandelion? Your whipper bottom just can't make the sardine this morning."

"Why was I thrice rejected?" asked the Dandelion. Hot pot anger boiled beneath the snatch, hidden and scarred by a mountain of tulips.

Dandelion whacked the tulip with his thirteenth bicep.

A Meeting With Soviet Steve

The sun rises across the Bering Straits of barren personality. It whits and whimpers, scattering from side to side, barreling along the infested and convoluted highway towards the arctic Tundra and the flat Pinelands of Siberia. Cold and wet, festooned with dromedary etchings, this camel-laden, lump of watery shit, this pile of personality in a bag, a screwball wedged between pillars of steel and lumps of plasterboard caked with wet coal and molasses sunk in deep-hued purple, this canvas sack filled with wet personality now rides, slides, and glides across the tundra oblivious to psychotherapy, and howling of distant wolves, and steel-jawed bear traps ogling the walking ego with each eye.

Stripped of its search warrant, the wayward personality slings shit from a starboard container, shooting from vast mangonels its heaving and heavy lumps of coal-black shit high in the virgin forests of Siberia.

"Can a medieval fortress ever survive in a delicatessen?" asked Lumpen Proletariat, the Stalin linchpin of former Soviet delis.

"Never could, and never will," answered Soviet Steve, grand stevedore of Grey's Anatomy. His heavy hide and bulbous legs crossed the festive waters beyond the Kamchatka Peninsula with wide, wild bell bottoms. "And what's so interesting about Siberia, anyway?"

Steve's beady Soviet-style eyes narrowed into Lumpen deilicatessen cornea; he bore, in wolf's clothing, the cornucopia of better time bombs exploding beyond sanctuary waters. "Can't you see the Soviet Union never worked?"

Although he spoke them with a forcefulness reserved for the Malachopski prisoners, these were definitely not Steve's words. Far behind, hidden in a closet behind a pine tree, perched just north of the equator, stood his mother. From her ubiquitous mouth shot moths of steel. Her wooden perch was camouflaged by pine trees, pine cones, and pine needles. She prickled as Rome burned. "Indeed, my son," she bellowed in long-drawn minnow tones, "you are flesh of my flesh. Better yet, you are fin of my fin (though none of us are Finnish), and scale of my scale. Indeed you are the finest flower and flour of Soviet fish I could ever imagine or hope would be born of my long-suffering, Duma-rotten 1905 Revolution, cold-pressed Lithuanian flesh."

An injected entity floored the piston near the floor. Lumpen Proletariat jumped up for air. "What about me?" he cried as he landed flat on a pre-Stalin turnip. "Can't you see I count, too? What about twins? I want equal protection under the law, and if I can't have it I'm going back under my bed."

"Such a whiner," screamed Mom from her new ice-capped home above the White Sea just east of Murmansk. "I can't wait until the sun sets. Then I can just whop you one giant Lenin-sized, back-fisted, post-Trotsky wallop, and none of the anti-spanking police will see me. You deserve it, you lumpen shithead! You were nothing but a downtrodden worm worker, anyway. Who needed you in the revolution, worthless piece of trash? Oh sure, you gave garbage workers something to carry, namely yourself. But where would they bring you, anyway? Perhaps to the Chernobyl nuclear dump to join the other delicatessen specialties like roast lamb of Jew, Jesus Christian liverwarts, diehard Mohammeds with their flatbread Sunni Allah Aloha hoppers from Hawaii, Shiite Fatimids from medieval Egypt, or a baked can of German worms from Wurms."

"Mother, you're being rather hard on him," squeaked Soviet Steve from his floating playpen now heading toward Irkutsk via Lake Baikal. "A little tolerance wouldn't hurt here."

But Mother lifted a neolithic tree from beneath the Asian continent and smashed Soviet Steve on the head with such force that communism crumbled.

Removing Seeds from Arthritic Joints

Reading the first line splits the sum and engenders flying eggballs. None can withstand boomersnitching on Friday morning. But it is Thursday. How can Boomer Snitcherhagen, first sister to crown prince Beaumont Heiny Peedelhofer hope to byswitch his German background? Are there really so many germs in Germ-any? Such a dangerous country is inhabited by both little and big Germ ans.

Nevertheless, one cannot easily snitch on Ludwig von Switcherhof or is brother Larry von Snitcherpoodle. That great court delicatessen of a man, swaggering north and south with with walrus teeth protruding recht und links from his pristine-but- putrid-purely-pulverized belly, could never lie beneath an accountant's count. In the duchy of his need, community serfs named him as their personal account ant. He had six legs and like to live in a hill. So did all his account ant friends. They related with deep feeling to local rodents. Insects, too. Indeed, among the Fourmis, an ancient sect of six-legged crawlers, accountant skills were deeply admired by both ants and uncles. Two centuries later, during the degeneration period of the meddle ages, accounting became popular among spiders, caterpillars, and butterflies.

Which reminds me of Madame Butterfly. Was she really Hungarian? Was she really the queen of Visegrad, the flying Pillangókisasszony of the Danube?

The ditributaries of each closure can rarely be met in such a fix. During the Meddling Ages, most inhabitants of the Bromide, the itinerant town of Pickleworth, knew this. So did Bentworth Higgins, the primogenture proprietor of Special Fruits Inc. Be careful about meeting him in a dark alley. Bentworth is a total fruit man; his limited commitment to vegetables is outstripped by fine furniture. Nevertheless, upon reading the Broccoli Chronicles, a seminal work co-written in Florida by the Seminole Indian, Hightower Magnolia of the competing firm of Fine Fruits of the Future, a realistic picture of Jason True Fruit, father and founder of of True Fruits, Inc. emerges.

Jason loved to hammer seeds into rock beds. He did this during morning ablutions in the town of Hammer Sledge Upon Rye located just south of a Pumpernickel Strip Joint. Here all seeds were removed from arthritic joints as well.

Camouflage walks in tilted towers tonight. The black haw of gammons gone wild can no longer sink the sleek Danube ships sailing by my window. A canister filled with leaded bombs goes off in the street below. Ants run for cover as do meat heads, purple marmalades, and insect features of the Third Reich. Can I help it if I Heil my way to pansy street scenes and fairy god mothers quacking in their duck boots, stringing peas of porridge pots across the goulash Hortobagy Hungarian plains while strong male antlers shriek for cover?

"I can't stand myself!" Laszlo Putrid, Hungarian son of the Japanese painter Sushi Vomit sinks his toe into a bowl of Chinese landworm soup. Then, turning his backside towards the pristine ceiling sky he farts into the sun. Soon his personalized rocket program is born and he receives a Fundament Foundation grant from the government.

"Koszonom szepen. Thank you." Laszlo squeezes the syllables

past his freshly brushed tooth. The wigwam whitewash worked. Rinsing his mouth with turpentine to remove the black paint stains, he bows deeply to the wall behind him, then blurts out in a burp. "I can't stand it but I love it!"

This morning he must visit his therapist, Sig Fried Laydown. Most of his session are held on a stove. He lies down in his frying pan.

"How do you feel this morning my little Heil Pooper," asks the kindly doctor. "Are your hemorrhoids heiling in the proper manner? Do they stand attention to salute the friendly SS sodium solution gendarmes that so kindly push them in with their solid Reich rifle butts?"

The Wild Whirlwind

Jack Pfeffer began the day in a stone. Why he couldn't read? There was also the question of his name. Was he really Jack Pfeffer? Or would Jack Pfiegelheiltzer do? What about his wife, Mary the Magnificent? Would she accepts stones? Or would simple laundry mold her life into the Cobbleskill crystal that so bemoaned her virgin state?

What about his goal to write a incomprehensible novel? One totally beyond understanding? Would he achieve this before his death? And if he didn't, why let death stop him? After all, he was a Stewperhoffer, born of aristocratic litter, bred in a pan, dumped in stew of sweatfire, created in the purple marmalade onion tube, the womb of all former Stewperhoffer's. Even his sister agreed.

Names never gave a bang, anyway.

"Mary," he called from his Tweeelet where he sat daily with dewhicky beedlehop mind scum, meditating upon a pie. "Are the turnips still frying?"

"Yes, dear," tweeted his wife, knitting her brow into a sweater. "I'll turn my skirt for you later."

Her womanly way, long refined by her Manor bred life shifting manure and sifting merchants from minor scale melodic cow farts, cued her life. Memories of the farm drifting through the ramparts of her fertile mind. Ah, Fart-Cow Manor as her parents called it, friendly home of adjacent cattle where toads roamed free and bicycles open their eyes to the lovely sun of blue sky heavens whose stewship barnsides had gone wild with hayseed. Such memories were not easily forgotten. Gently, she turned the turnips in the pan.

"It'll be ready in a jiffy, darling" she called. Jack sat stone still upon his toilet meditating over chewed porridge. "Breakfast is coming."

"It is the wild thing to do," quoth Lancelot, the next character in this drama. He picked up his pig behind the barn.

"A quick trip into the past, eh?" asked Jack, his perpin-penguined eyelids twinkling askew on his head. His wide-birthed mothers of Toms River stropped sidewards. "It is time to warry the plen." He broked his jaw. "What of Perpignan or the French Riviera? Won't those faucets of ancient Roman culture ever jump the line?"

"Not on your life," answered Lancelot. "Besides, they have narry a til to do with Roman estuaries since their midst are mere Corfu conglomerates in a Corsican sky. Can't you keep your histories straight?"

Jack wiggled his superior toe nail. "Are you such a historian? Can your weedle, histogenic, backwards sinking brain ever freely accommodate historitudes? Who cares about Corsica anyway? I am not Ajaccian. Nor do I give a shit about Napoleon or Elba."

Lancelot placed his calloused hand upon the swine back at his side. Then, popping a piglet, he spoke in dulcet long-winded, hyperbolic, strobococcic, mercurial tones. Invoking the Roman gods Mars and Mercury, he strobicated: "Cur of an onion! Can't you see the wont and wanton twisting of your ways? Roman culture cannot be dampened by such turnip minds as yours. Let us drop the subject before my hind quarters start to vent."

Lancelot clasped his hands as he walked together with the other parts of his mind towards the parlor of Martha the Magnificent. Speaking in unison with his many selves, "they" said: "We'll speak about this in the parlor."

A bleak sky, beaked with uncertitude trembled above him. A Great Force in lordly framework, dressed in stunning wolf's clothing leaned down, bending towards Lancelot and Jack. Deep serpentine grumbled. Words of reassurance rolled, awe struck and with thunder, spread speeding through the green-grass universe as bass voice boomed: "Where are the loins of yesteryear?"

"Hark," speckled Lancelot. "Can it be the Lord Himself bending low, speaking to us?"

Jack looked up and down. "I see no one. Nor do I hear any vibration."

"Indeed, your inner life is wanting," quoth the peripatetic pig farmer. "Lack of Latin and Greek cognates has squabbled your squelched-rotted mind. This lucklack hole of fortune enables you to only hear pagan words. Divinity falls short as shadows of porcupine silt hide your spiritual life."

Jack's eyes drifted into a hollow mire of mirthlessness.

Can cantaloupes simmer in dewdrops? We'll never know says Louie the Turnip, emblem keeper of the hogwash stewardship.

Should a date stride the top of such belittling understew? I doubt it, said Purgy. I think yes, said Pensive. This battle of subwits continued on til doomsday. But a final decision was made. Today will be date day; tomorrow we will see.

"Well, who cares about such ninitudes?" quoth the venerable Homer. "Truth is, I was down in the dumps last night. The TV screen reeked my brain and smashed it to bits. I ended up sleeping in a dust bin. This is no way to end or begin the day. Discipline, my friend. Well, what does that mean? Sticking to the tried and narrow will not necessarily open the spring of my brain nor feed the canting estuaries therein. No, discipline is a natural phenomenon. It comes from riding the feeling to the end, seeing where the fucker leads. Discipline? Fuck it. Follow the feeling. Whether it leads down into the gutter or up to heaven is really besides the point. Up or down, back or forth, ultimately they are both the same. Mainly I want the route of adventure! And following the path of feeling leads to the ultimate adventure. Yes, treading the path deep into self. That is the adventure par excellence."

"Well, Homer, that is very nice of you to say." Leslie Turnip von Pubenhoffen stood in the doorway of her wigwam, leaning on the Sioux Indian sill and smoking a long view Appalachian cigarette. Her strong North Dakota accent bent the sterile winds from the plain around her.

"Following feelings is fine, "she said. "But what about Torah. . . or even Talmud? What Sioux or even Redfox Indian can feel complete without daily reading of these wigwam leaves? Don't you think constant and disciplined daily study on a gay and daily basis will bring the essence of rednecks home to roost?"

"Strange," said the Lancelot Indian. "I miss my Jewish phase. But it seems as dead as it can be. I can no longer mourn it or believe it. Perhaps it is best to put it aside for awhile, to forget it, let it sink in. Does this mean I move into Indian and Sanskrit texts? Or does all philosophy, self-searching, and religious literature go into the dust bin? For awhile, of course and no doubt. But there I am today.

Rebellion!: More Conversations with Ma

Larry Bentworth knew the time had come. Death stalked his very prey and this in his back yard. The vast swirl of peremptory sky wandered overhead. Mother was talking and it wasn't sweet talk either.

"Get on the high road!" she squawked. Her wide-mouth banter lite up the purple sky, dampening the Holland Tunnel as she went. "Yes, this high road, Larry, my son." She bent her finger to the wind. "You cannot squiggle and drippulate nor wander in this seepid morass of self-squandry. Am I making myself clear? A firm voice is needed here and it is mine. Left on your own you simply dribble into dintworthship. Daily slipping and sliding into the grave is no way to live. It is simply not a good attitude. And indeed, I see you slipping. You have forgotten most of what I have taught you. Run wild on the lawn? Ha. Why do you think you did it in the first place? To get away from me? Well, partly. But also to impress me. And sure, I told you to shut up, ship out, and quiet down. What's a good mother to do? Simply to let you shit in your pants all day is no highward task for a pruning, healthy, reaping, prulullating, and Bentworth mother. Why do you think we're called the Bentworths anyway? It is because we a bent worth, our bends are worthy, we strike a blend of upmanship in this often downward moving world. And I will make you worthy whether you like it or not! That is my task. And that is why you both cannot and must run wild on the lawn. Who, after all, do you think is composing this Wild Whirlwind anyway? You? Ha. Only your fingers are moving. But crawling in your mind, deep behind your eyes and even often close to the surface is your good old mother. I will never leave you. Nor can you ever get away. Nor should you. But always you will and must push, push, push. Push what and against whom? Why me, of course. I am the wall against which you test your pushing strength. I am your growth wall. Did you think you could lose me through mere therapy? Who created your miracle schedule after all? It was I. And after that it was me, me, me.

"I am important to you for many reasons. Nay, not only important, but vital! You cannot live without me. I am so deeply embedded in your brain that only a total lobotomy can remove me. In fact, upon further reflection, even that is not enough. Only a trip to the guillotine could do it. Total removal of the head is the only way to go. Sure, death follows. But without me, you are dead anyway. The only difference is that you would still be walking around. But whether you join the living dead, the walking dead, or the lying dead, dead is dead. It is not the place for my son to me. My son will never die! I simply won't allow it. No, no, no! You will live forever and that is that!"

"But, Ma," said Larry as he sat in his underwear, the New York Times beneath his feet. "Why did I spend all that time and money in therapy if I can't and, as you say, shouldn't get rid of you? What about cure? What is cure? What does it mean, anyway?"

"Cure, my son, is discovering your rebellious side. You are supposed to, among other things, rebel against me. And this, despite what all those fucking Buddhists say about love and compassion for your fellow man. Fuck that shit. Now you might say this is no way for a mother to talk but I am no ordinary mother. I am your mother!

"How will you going to rise above the ordinary? Through the energy of rebellion. How and why should you follow and fulfill the dictates of that miracle schedule you invented? To rise above the ordinary, of course. And what is the ordinary but the level, leveling, depressing, status quo of mundane life. The desert of this existence is no place for an artist. And you, my son, are an artist! That is your essence and nature. I didn't daily push your head in the toilet just so you could be like everyone else. I wanted you to know shit, and know it well, so that "others would never be able to call you a shithead."

"But they all did, Ma."

"Of course they did. But they were the outsiders, the wandering shadows walking past that beautiful imagination chamber of your mind, the artistic room in which you lived your daily, vital, wild fantasy, brilliant imaginings, death-defying, whirlwind life. Symbolized by ecstatic violin flights, this room, believe it not, was created for you by me!"

"You? I created it to get away from you."

"Precisely. That's why I bugged, pestered, rode, and haunted you; that's why I beat your public brain into a pulp. So you could retreat into the private world of your imagination and create great artistic works. Who ever heard of an artist living in public. If you live in public you become a lawyer or politician, or maybe, on a higher level, even a teacher. But no matter what you do in public without the existence of your steadfast pillar, the creative chamber of your imagination, you can never amount to anything. Public life is a mere reflection of that. First the world is created and imagined in your mind. Then it is shit out, through mouth and anus, and becomes public property; it fertilizes the fair grounds beyond your room. Public service? Ha! That's okay. But without the creations of your private laboratory, the miracles constructed in the violin room of your imagination, the public works you dump in the grounds beyond your chamber would truly be mere shit."

Larry pondered long and deep. "You mean I have to credit you for pushing me back into my room?"

"Damn right."

"Spoken like a true mother. I'll have to think about all this."

Just Do What You're Told!

Mary asked Hector: "What did God tell you?"

Hector answered in pensive tone. "He said "Shut up!" Then gave His ultimate commandment: Serve me with joy. . . or else!"

"You're quite a theologian, Hector. Can you expound upon this loving doctrine a bit more?"

"Ain't much love on the surface here. It's way in the background. Lots of push, though, lots of pressure to enjoy yourself. Without joy, you ain't really worshiping.

"You mean it's a order? I gotta enjoy myself?"

"Damn right."

"What a downer."

"Shut up. Follow your orders. Joy is tough. But it's a commandment. Like I said, just do what you're told. Get on the magnificence, glory, awe, and wonder road. Otherwise forget it."

www.ingramcontent.com/pod-product-compliance
Lightning Source LLC
Chambersburg PA
CBHW070656100426
42735CB00039B/2160